The Outrageous Love of God

Other titles by Herb Hodges:

Tally Ho the Fox!
The Foundation for Building World-Visionary,
World-Impacting, Reproducing Disciples

Fox Fever
Exploring both the Will and the Skill to obey Christ's
Great Commission to "turn people into disciples."

Available from: Spiritual Life Ministries
2916 Old Elm Lane
Germantown, TN 38138
901-758-2777
E-mail: herbslm@mindspring.com

DOWN THE MINISTRIES
6071 WALNUT GROVE RD
STE 410
MEMPHIS, TN 38120
901 685 5277

Merchant ID: 80160?2194
Term ID: 000?9200080160?2194006

Sale

xxxxxxxxxxxx7259
MASTERCARD   Entry Method: Swiped

Total: $ 13.00

2/19/11   10:47:39
Inv #: 000011   Appr Code: 003788
pprvd: Online

Customer Copy

THANK YOU

The
Outrageous
Love
of God

A series

of studies

on the

'Pearl of

the Parables'   **Herb Hodges**

The Outrageous Love of God

Herb Hodges, author

All Scripture quotations, unless otherwise indicated, are taken from
the King James Version.

On the cover: *The Return of the Prodigal Son* by Pompeo Batoni, 1773.

Spiritual Life Ministries
2616 Old Elm Lane
Germantown, TN 38138
901-758-2777
E-mail: herbslm@mindspring.com

ISBN: 978-0-9788201-7-6

Printed in the United States of America

Published by IMD Press
7140 Hooker Street
Westminster, CO 80030
www.imdpress.com

Contents

Introduction

The story of the prodigal son is regarded by most people as the greatest story Jesus ever told. I would add the proviso of my own conviction—that Luke 15, the entire chapter of lost things, though seemingly made of four stories (sheep, silver coin, prodigal son and elder brother), is actually all one story in which each segment of the story adds a significant and indispensable part of the whole. The last chapter in this small book is an attempt to view the parts and their integration into the whole message Jesus presented in this brilliant parable.

Each time I contact this great chapter of the Word of God, God gets "up close and personal" with fresh assurances of His love and grace. I see myself as the helpless, overmatched sheep in the wilderness, totally dependent on the heart and effort of Jesus, the seeking shepherd. I see myself as the valuable but displaced "coin" which commandeers the attention and search of the blessed Holy Spirit. I see myself as the young rebel who was willing to abuse his father to get his own way, and as the arrogant older brother who expressed his Pharisaic heart in claiming that he had earned the right to be his father's favorite. But most of all, I am overwhelmed by the seeking, searching, suffering heart of the great God of love, the Father of the Forever Family of God's children, who has extravagantly given Himself to reach and receive and restore His lost property and personnel. I see the Father's heart swelling with compassion and love for errant sinners like myself, and I am overwhelmed again with the great Romance of the Gospel.

In fact, I easily see all three Persons of the Triune God, the Father, the Son and the Holy Spirit in this complete story. The shepherd is an accurate portrait of Jesus the Son of God, the seeker and Savior of desperately lost sinners. The woman seeking the coin suggests the Holy Spirit on a crusade at home to locate that which is strangely lost inside the Owner's house. The loving, compassionate "prodigal" Father represents God the Father, who sponsors even rebel man with "common grace," which man repays by rebellious and riotous living indulged at the Father's expense. The retrieving shepherd, the retrieving woman in the house and the receiving Father who welcomes His son from the far country—each represents God in another facet of His glorious grace.

In an enlightening chapter about idolatry (Psalm 115), the Bible tells us that when people worship a god, they tend to become like the god they worship. What a different world this would be if people would focus on the God revealed in Luke fifteen so that they finally emerge bearing His likeness. "We all, beholding as in a mirror the glory of the Lord (Jesus), are changed into the same image from glory to glory, even as by the Spirit of the Lord" (II Corinthians 3:18, my all-time life's motto verse). I pray that you will see the clear Image of the God of prodigal love as you read these pages. Using us, His children, as His stage of action, may God flood the world again with His outrageous love.

The Outrageous Love of God

The Lost Sheep
Luke 15:1-7

I. The Pitiful Picture of a Lost Sheep
      A. Spiritually dumb

      B. Spiritually drifting

      C. Spiritually defenseless

II. The Powerful Picture of a Loving Shepherd
      A. Personal sympathy

      B. Persistent seeking

      C. Practical self-sacrifice

III. The Perfect Picture of a Lasting Salvation
      A. Entirely by grace

      B. Entirely through faith

      C. Provides perfect security

The Lost Sheep

Luke 15:1-7

Then drew near unto Him all the publicans and sinners for to hear Him. And the Pharisees and scribes murmured, saying, This man receiveth sinners, and eateth with them. And He spake this parable unto them, saying, What man of you, having a hundred sheep, if he lose one of them, doth not leave the ninety and nine in the wilderness, and go after that which is lost, until he find it? And when he hath found it, he layeth it on his shoulders, rejoicing. And when he cometh home, he calleth together his friends and neighbors, saying unto them, Rejoice with me; for I have found my sheep which was lost. I say unto you, that likewise joy shall be in heaven over one sinner that repenteth, more than over ninety and nine just persons, which need no repentance.

The fifteenth chapter of Luke's Gospel is not a series of parables as we are normally told that it is. It is all one parable. "Jesus spoke *this* parable unto them," verse three says. And each successive part of the parable begins with a connecting word. There is no indication whatever of a second or third parable in this chapter, only one. Also, there are not three parts to the parable, but four. And there are not three lost things in the chapter, but four. In fact, the one which we don't consider as lost is, in fact, *so* lost that when the parable closes, he is the only one who *remains* lost. Indeed, the elder brother represents the scribes and Pharisees who provoked Jesus to tell the parable to begin with (verses 1-3).

The first two parts of the parable argue from man to God. "What man of you." "Either what woman." So Jesus asks His audience to declare what they would do if this situation were to arise in their lives—that is, if each of them was either the shepherd or the woman in the story. What shepherd in this situation would not act in this manner? What woman in this situation would not act in this manner? There is tremendous genius in this manner of speech; it disarms His critics by forcing them to admit that they would act the same way if faced with the same necessity.

"What shepherd, having a hundred sheep, if he lose one of them, ...?" The loss in this case is one percent, a very small and relatively insignificant loss. So the motive for finding the lost object in this part of the story is *not profit for the owner*, but *pity for the object*. We have only to compare the second part of the parable with the story of the sheep to see this clearly. In the second part, the woman had ten coins and lost one of them. So the loss is much more substantial and significant. For a businessman to lose ten percent of his assets would be a sizeable loss. So the motive for seeking and repossessing the lost object in the second part is the profit of the owner. It is *"sheep-interest"* that motivates the shepherd; it is *self-interest* that motivates the woman who lost the one coin. What a world of reality lies behind these insights! Incidentally, the motive for recovery in the third and fourth parts of the story is the passion of the father for his two sons. To lose a sheep is one thing, to lose a coin is another, but to lose even a single son is unbearable to a true father.

The shepherd "leaves the ninety and nine in the wilderness (in a sheepfold) and goes after that which is lost." And when he finds the lost sheep, "he came home." What a peculiarity! We would expect the shepherd to take the found sheep back to the sheepfold, but he doesn't. He takes it "home." Why? Because he wanted celebrators to enjoy the rescue with him, but sheep cannot celebrate. So he went home where he could "call his friends and neighbors together, saying to them, Rejoice with me, for I have found my sheep which was lost." Do you see the heart of God? Each part of this parable presents as a major theme God's celebration over the recovery of a lost person.

One reason so few lost people are saved in many churches is that the church is generally indifferent to the great rescue when it occurs. A lost person comes trusting Christ as Lord and Savior, and declaring that he has been delivered from hell and is on his way to heaven with Christ in his heart—and we yawn from too little sleep on Saturday night, consult our watches to be sure the service doesn't go five minutes overtime without our protest, and wonder if our roast is burning (of if we will get caught in the heavy line at the cafeteria)! So God quits going to church where we go. He goes somewhere where He can enlist celebrators! Also, the word "home" indicates another great spiritual truth. It reveals that a redeemed sinner regains more through

The Outrageous Love of God

his salvation than Adam lost for us through his sin. "Home" over "sheepfold!" So it is far, far better to be a redeemed sinner than an innocent Adam. Jesus recovered far more for us than Adam lost for us.

Notice how familiar Jesus is, while on earth, with what is going on in heaven. "I say unto you that likewise joy shall be in heaven over one sinner that repenteth more than over ninety and nine just persons which need no repentance." Also, why does Jesus include the word "repent" twice in the explanatory verse that is not even really a part of the story? Because there is no repentance in the story otherwise. Sheep cannot repent, but sinners cannot get to heaven without it, so Jesus *adds* it to complete the account. The same is true in the second part of the story, also. Coins cannot repent, so Jesus adds this dimension of the Gospel message to the story (verse 10). It might be added that it was not necessary for Jesus to add repentance to the third and fourth parts of the story because *boys can* repent, and one does (the prodigal) and one doesn't (the elder brother) in the last parts of the story. So repentance is built into those last two parts, and thus it was not necessary for Jesus to add it to those parts of the story.

Look with me at the story of the lost sheep. Let me divide the picture into three parts.

I. The Pitiful Picture of a Lost Sheep

I want you to think, first, of *the pitiful picture of a lost sheep.* License your imagination.

The shepherd brought his large flock of sheep back to the wilderness sheepfold one evening after a day's journeying to forage for grass and water. He stood with his staff in his hand as his sheep broke into single file to enter the narrow opening into the sheepfold. As they entered, he touched the head of each sheep with his staff and counted that sheep. "Ninety-one, ninety-two, ninety-three, ninety-four, ninety-five, ninety-six, ninety-seven, ninety-eight, *ninety-nine....*" Suddenly, everything in him went rigid. You see, there is hardly anything more pitiable on earth than a single sheep wandering without a shepherd in a wilderness. It's only a matter of time before it will be destroyed. The shepherd quickly thinks back over the day and wonders where the sheep might have become lost. Everything in the shepherd goes into active alert, because one of his sheep was "lost" (verses 4, 6). What does this part of the story tell us of the meaning of the word "lost?" Can we tell from a sheep what is true of human beings? Yes, we can.

First, to be lost means to be *spiritually dumb.* Aubrey Johnston, the representative of Friends For Wildlife of the southwestern United States, said, "If you could take all the brains of all the sheep in all the world and put them into the skull of one sheep, you just might have a reasonably intelligent animal." A sheep is the dumbest animal on the face of the earth. And who is Jesus talking about? Us! You and me! Human beings, both saved and lost, are like sheep. All of our intuitive and natural understanding, coupled with all our natural learning, is so much *spiritual stupidity*!

The Outrageous Love of God

Do you remember the story of Samson when he fell into the hands of the Philistines? They took a white-hot poker and burned his eyes out of his head, and he was stone blind for the rest of his life. Well, when Adam fell into the hands of Satan, Satan put out his eyes spiritually. "If our Gospel be hid (veiled or covered), it is hid to them that are lost: In whom the god of this world (Satan) has blinded the minds of them which believe not, lest the light of the glorious Gospel of Christ, who is the image of God, should shine unto them" (II Corinthians 4:3, 4). So every man today, being a child of Adam, is born blind to the things of God. He is spiritually dumb and *will remain so unless he receives the miracle of Divine sight.* He cannot understand anything that really matters without a miracle. Sin has such a stupefying and stultifying power in human life that it makes its victim absolutely ignorant, senseless, and dumb to Divine truth and reality. And there are no exceptions, exemption, or exclusions to this rule— without a Divine miracle.

How many trained sheep have you ever seen? Have you ever seen a trained sheep in a circus? You may see trained dogs, trained cats, trained horses, trained elephants, trained lions and tigers, but you have never seen a trained sheep. A leading London pastor went down to dockside where a load of sheep were being brought off a ship from New Zealand. The sheep were coming down a single-file chute and loading onto a truck. The pastor secured permission to make an experiment. He put a rod across the unloading chute, and the sheep quickly backed up in the chute. Then the first sheep jumped over the rod, then the second, the third, the fourth, and the fifth. Then the pastor removed the rod—and the sheep kept jumping. In Thomas Hardy's classic story, *Far From the Madding Crowd*, when the rowdy dog started the sheep over the cliff, he then could stand and watch, because they would dumbly follow the leader to their deaths. Ephesians 4:18 tells us that lost men are "alienated from the life of God through the *ignorance* that is in them."

Many flocks of sheep have a lead sheep which is call a "bellwether." All the sheep will follow this leader—regardless of outcome. The human race has a "bellwether." His name is Adam. By his sin, he set the direction and destination of the whole human race. And each man agrees with Adam's choice by his own sins. Because we are blind, we don't even know what is wrong.

Second, to be lost means to be *spiritually drifting* without direction. Isaiah 53:6 says, "All we *like sheep* have *gone astray*. We have turned every man to his own way." This is the primary and all-determinative truth about every lost person on earth. I Peter 2:25 says, "You were as sheep going astray." Notice the important difference in these two verses. In the first, the sheep has "*gone* astray;" it is away from the shepherd and lost. In the second, the sheep is "*going* astray." This means that each step the sheep takes carries it farther from the shepherd's care and safety. Both of these are true of lost people. They are "lost" when they are without Christ, but in one tragic sense, they become "more lost" each day they remain without Christ. Their direction is wrong, the distance increases between them and the shepherd, and they have no equipment for finding their way back. No lost sinner ever drifts to Jesus! In fact, no person ever *drifts* to *any place* that is worth going to. A sheep has no sense of direction. A lost horse may find its way back to the corral, and many other lost animals may find their way back home. We know of the "homing pigeon," but we have never heard of a "homing sheep." The only genius of a sheep is to get himself lost. And Jesus is talking here about you and me!

Someone said, "The word 'evil' is simply the word 'live' spelled backwards." So what is sin? It is *life going in the wrong direction*—away from Jesus, the Good Shepherd. Peter spoke of his generation as an "untoward generation," a generation not going toward a proper goal. Where is hell? It is *at the end of the life of the person who never stops to look where he is going*. An old crazy story told of an airline pilot who radioed to his passengers and said, "Ladies and gentlemen, I have bad news and good news. The bad news is, we're lost! The good new is, we're making good time!" Most moderns are "making good time"—right straight toward hell! And many also stupidly and arrogantly refuse the corrective advances of those whose eyes have been opened and whose direction has been forever changed from hell to heaven. So men are just like lost sheep—spiritually drifting and too dumb to know it or correct it.

Third, to be lost is to be *spiritually defenseless*. A sheep has no means of personal defense. A dog can bite, a cat can scratch, a horse can kick, a deer can run, a squirrel can climb, a turtle can retire into its shell, a skunk.... I heard of a mother skunk who took her family of little skunks to church one Sunday. When they arrived, she said, "Let us *spray*." And it was so terrible that each went and sat in his own *pew!* That wasn't worth a *scent*, was it? But what can a sheep do to defend itself? A sheep isn't prepared for fight or for flight. It can't run fast or far. It can't ford water. It can't leap or climb easily. Its jaws are so weak that it doesn't normally bite off grass; it pulls it up by the roots. This is what created the range wars in the early western United States. So a sheep is completely without defense. If a lion were to spy out a lost sheep, or a wolf were to cross its track, or a bear, it would be totally at the mercy of the beast of prey.

Even so, a lost man is defenseless against the spiritual powers that oppose him. "Be serious, be watchful, because your Adversary the Devil, like a roaring lion, walks about, seeking whom he may devour" (I Peter 5:8). That verse is incorporated at the end of a passage about flocks of sheep and a chief shepherd. What chance would a helpless, unprotected sheep have against a vicious roaring lion? That's how much chance every lost person has against the destructive attacks of sin, Satan, and even the wrath of God against sin which "abides upon" every lost person (John 3:36; Romans 1:18). Unless the shepherd comes to his aid, it is only a matter of time until he is totally destroyed.

So the person without Christ is pathetically lost—spiritually dumb, spiritually drifting, and spiritually defenseless.

Now, let's see the second picture presented in this tiny story.

II. The Powerful Picture of a Loving Shepherd

The second picture in this part of the parable is *the powerful picture of a loving shepherd*. There is absolutely no doubt as to the spiritual identity of the shepherd in this story. In John 10:11, Jesus plainly said, "I am the Good Shepherd." In I Peter 2:25, Peter said to Christians, "You returned unto the Shepherd of your souls." David said, "The Lord is my shepherd" (Psalm 23:1). Then, what does this story tell us about Jesus?

First, He is an individual of *personal sympathy* toward each lost person. That shepherd was not unconcerned when he discovered that one sheep was lost. He was not apathetic or indifferent. He didn't say, "Oh, well, it's a minimal loss, only one of a hundred. And these sheep should really be more careful!" No! Everything in the Shepherd became alarmed over the lostness of the one sheep. In Matthew 9:36, we read that "when Jesus saw the multitudes, He was moved with compassion on them, because they fainted, and were scattered abroad, as sheep having no shepherd." The word "moved" is a very strong word; it could be translated "convulsed." The word "compassion" is a form of the Greek word for "bowels" or "intestines." In fact, the term is sometimes translated "bowels of compassion" in your New Testament. So Jesus was convulsively stirred by the sight of lost people. Does this sound like an indifferent, disinterested, or antagonistic person? The shepherd, like Jesus, became deeply implicated in the lostness of the dumb, drifting, defenseless object.

How important is one lost person to Jesus? On one occasion, He said, "Are not two sparrows sold for a penny?" Pretty worthless little creatures, aren't they? Later He said, "Are not five sparrows sold for two pennies?" The business dimension of His question reveals some interesting features. Mathematically, if two sparrows are sold for a penny, then reasonably, four sparrows should be sold for two pennies. But no, a merchant will add a little volume to entice a larger sale. That fifth sparrow is tossed in as an incidental item to him. But Jesus said that never does a single sparrow fall from the sky without the Heavenly Father's eye being upon it. *God attends a sparrow's funeral!* Then He lovingly said, "And are not you of much greater value than many, many sparrows?" Dear lost sinner, you mean a great deal to God! And remember, His motive at this point is not profit to Himself, but pity for you.

Second, this Shepherd is an individual of *persistent seeking.* He "goes after that which is lost, until he finds it" (Luke 15:4). This story matches one lone shepherd against an entire vast wilderness. But, regardless of how small he seems or how large the search area, he is not coming back "until he finds the thing that is lost."

Christianity is the only religion on earth in which *God* seeks *man.* In all other religions (approximately twelve might be called "world" religions), man seeks God (which is like a bridge solidly connected at man's end, but totally washed out at the other, God's end, and thus no contact can be made). Only in Christianity has God come to man "to seek and to save that which was lost" (Luke 19:10).

Francis Thompson wrote a great poem entitled "The Hound of Heaven," an incredible picture of Jesus, the expert tracker, pursuing the lost sinner, who is hurrying on without direction away from the destiny and the destination he was made for. Listen to some of the "sheep speech" of his insightful poem:

I fled Him, down the nights and down the days;
I fled Him, down the arches of the years;
I fled Him, down the labyrinthine ways
Of my own mind; and in the midst of tears
I hid from Him, and under running laughter.

On I fled and on I sped
From those strong Feet that followed, followed after.
But with unhurrying chase, And undisturbed pace,
Deliberate speed, majestic instancy,
They beat—and a Voice beat More instant than the Feet:
"All things betray thee, who betrayest Me."

Each succeeding section closes with a powerful punch line from the Shepherd: *"Nothing shelters you, who will not shelter Me." "Nothing contents you, who will not content Me."* And the poem closes with these final words:

The shade of His hand is outstretched caressingly,
"Ah, fondest, blindest, weakest,

I am He Whom thou seekest!

Thou drovest love from thee, who drovest Me."

Thompson's poem combines the ideas of Jesus' parable: a beloved, but blind and weak creature, stupidly moving steadily away from its only Savior and its only salvation. But the Savior, the Good Shepherd, keeps coming deeper and deeper into the wilderness—"until he finds it." How do you measure the word "until"? You must *go to Bethlehem*, and see the Miracle Baby of Miracle Birth, come with the Miracle Blessing. "Unto you is born this day in the city of David a *Savior*, who is Christ the Lord." And you must *go to Judea* and hear Him speak "as never man spake" and see Him act like no ordinary man has ever acted. Then, you must *go to Jerusalem* and see Him raised on a Cross between Heaven and earth as if He were fit for neither, and then see Him *raised again—this time from the dead!* And all this *for you!*

On a green Hill far away, Outside a city wall,

The dear Lord was crucified, Who died to save us all.

If you are to understand the word "until," you must trace both His outward journey to repossess that which was lost, and His return journey in saving and fully securing it to its final destination.

But none of the ransomed ever knew,

How deep were the waters crossed,

Or how dark was the night that the Lord passed through,

Ere He found His sheep that was lost.

The Outrageous Love of God

Like a sleuthhound, Jesus follows the sheep—across mountain steep and through valley deep, tracing all its windings and wanderings and waywardness—*"until."* He is a person of persistent seeking.

Third, this Shepherd is an individual of *practical self-sacrifice.* Again, consider the word "until." The motivation of that word carried him through the darkness of the night, through the threat of the wilderness, through the attack of beasts, through blood-letting and bruises of briars, thorns, rocks, crags, and any other impediments between him and the safety of the sheep. In John 10:11, Jesus said, "I am the Good Shepherd; the Good Shepherd giveth His life for the sheep." The word "for" in that statement is the preposition, "huper," which means "over." The shepherd throws himself protectively "over" the sheep or between the sheep and any attacker. Anything that would attack the sheep must dispose of the shepherd first. And the sheep is warranted to hide behind the shepherd when an enemy approaches.

Between my sins and their reward,

I set the death of Christ my Lord.

When Abe Lincoln's funeral procession was moving through Springfield, Illinois, it is said that a Negro woman, a former slave, held up a Negro child and cried, "Take a long, long look, child, 'cause that's the man who died for you!" Dear lost man, lost woman, stop what you are doing, note the Shepherd's approach to you, and take a long, long look, because that's *The Man Who Died For You.*

Now, the last picture of this story.

III. The Perfect Picture of a Lasting Salvation

Finally, there is in this part of the parable *the perfect picture of a lasting salvation*. The real genius of the story fairly glares at us at this point. "When he hath found it, he layeth it on his shoulders, rejoicing. And when he cometh home, he calleth together his friends and neighbors, saying unto them, Rejoice with me; for I have found my sheep which was lost." What a glorious picture of God's great salvation of lost sinners!

First, God's salvation is *entirely by grace*. How much did the sheep do to save itself? Nothing! Did the sheep seek the shepherd? No, the shepherd sought the sheep! Did the sheep travel any of the distance between it and the shepherd? No, all the distance was crossed by the shepherd! Did the sheep leap up into the shepherd's arms? No, the shepherd lifted it up!

Gordon MacDonald was right when he called grace "the deepest and Divinest word of the Gospel." Someone wisely said, "Grace is the face God wears when He meets our imperfection, sin, waywardness, weakness, and failure." We may not be able to understand grace with our natural or carnal minds, but *the Bible will not allow us to negate or to neutralize its overwhelming message of grace*. The God of the Bible offers grace upon grace upon grace, "grace for grace," wave upon wave (John 1:16). The Bible tells us in no uncertain terms that the grace of God is the only thing there is that is bigger than sin. "Where sin abounded, grace super-abounded" (Romans 5:20). Our salvation is entirely by grace. "By grace are you saved through faith, and that not of yourselves (the source of your salvation is not in your person); it is the gift of God, not of works (the source of your salvation is not in your performance), lest any man should boast" (Ephesians 2:8-9). Now, stupid man resents losing his boast. That's incredible, isn't it? He resents not being able to handle his own case. He fights against the Benefactor who offers to sponsor him, and hugs his own poverty, helplessness, and damnation!

C. S. Lewis pictures this strange resentment masterfully in his little allegory, The Great Divorce, the story of the separation between those in heaven and those in hell. Lost souls are like ghosts because they have no weight and no substance. Saved people have various degrees of weight and substance, depending on how centered they became (during their lives on earth) on Jesus and others. In one scene, a lost person and a saved person are discussing their previous lives on earth. The lost person says, "I don't say that I was a religious man and I don't say I had no faults, far from it. But I done my best all my life, see? I done my best by everyone, that's the sort of chap I was. I never asked for anything that wasn't mine by rights. If I wanted a drink I paid for it and if I took my wages I done my job, see? That's the sort I was and I don't care who knows it." When the saved person declares that a sinner must give up his rights and totally trust a mighty, Divine Benefactor to save Him, the lost man protests, "I only want my rights. I'm not asking for anybody's bleeding charity." Listen to the saved man's response: "Then do. At once. Ask for the Bleeding Charity. Everything is here for the asking and nothing can be bought." To which the lost man replies, "I don't see myself going in the same boat with you, see? Why should I? I don't want charity. I'm a decent man and if I have my rights I'd have been in heaven long ago and you can tell them I said so." How blind, vain, and stupid a hopeless, helpless, homeless, hapless sinner must be to refuse the free gift of eternal life in favor of his own selfishness! Salvation is by grace. It is accomplished only by God's initiative, by God's work, and by God's power. If you get to Heaven, you will get there only by the sheer courtesy and goodwill of Almighty God.

Second, this salvation is through faith. We must remember that this story is only part of the full picture. We dare not look for a full description of faith in the story of a sheep or a coin (the second part of the story), because neither a sheep nor a coin can exercise faith. The other two parts of the story are required to furnish the full picture of faith. But we do have a good partial picture of faith here. What is faith as it is revealed here? It is a resting in Christ's hands, a relaxing in His care, a suspending of our full weight upon Him. Faith is "weighting" upon God! Faith means that I transfer my trust totally away from every other possibility and trust Jesus Christ totally to save me.

One little girl was asked, "Who saved you?" Her answer was rather startling. She said, "Me and God." "What do you mean, you and God?" "Why, God did the saving, and I did the letting." "Letting" is as effortless as any thing a human being can do. The sheep stopped squirming and straying, and let the shepherd do his job! Faith is not merely giving your assent; it is giving yourself.

Ralph Waldo Emerson once defined faith as "the rejection of a lesser fact and the acceptance of a greater fact." You are a lost sinner, and that is the greatest fact about you—until. When Jesus arrives, He and His accomplishment are recognized as a far greater fact. The acceptance of the overwhelming greater fact fairly obliterates the lesser fact. When your trust is transferred from all else and placed in Him, you become a saved person—through faith. "By grace are ye saved through faith."

Finally, this salvation provides perfect security for the saved. There are two things involved in the sheep's salvation once the shepherd has arrived. One is the shepherd's hands, and the other is the shepherd's shoulders. Incidentally, the word is plural, "shoulders" (verse 5), and this tells us volumes about God's salvation! This Shepherd's hands have never mishandled a single sinner. You are "in good hands with this Almighty Shepherd!" And this Shepherd's shoulders have never sagged under the weight of a single trusting sinner.

Not only are there two parts of the Shepherd involved immediately in this salvation—His hands and His shoulders; there are also five movements of the shepherd in behalf of the sheep in the story, and each provides a great insight into the salvation which Jesus secures for sinners.

First, the shepherd goes to the sheep. "The Son of Man has come to seek and save that which was lost" (Luke 19:10).

Second, the shepherd reaches down and lays hold of the sheep. Jesus the Shepherd reaches down to us through the powerful work of the Holy Spirit, and arrests us by His grace and power.

He "apprehends" us (Philippians 3:12) with two long arms, the long arm of His Law and the other long arm of His love.

Third, the shepherd lifts the sheep. Jesus lifts us up to association and identification with Himself. "He brought me up," said the Psalmist (Psalm 40:3). The word "brought" means that He came down into my situation, identified me with Himself, and took me back up with Him.

Fourth, the shepherd places the sheep on his shoulders. Friends, it is absolutely critical that we understand and emphasize this part of the story. Again, note that the word is "shoulders," and that it is plural. The usual picture that is painted of this story shows the shepherd in a pleasant pastoral scene, surrounded by other sheep, and carrying the sheep in his bosom. That is not what God's Word says! "He layeth it on his shoulders," Jesus said. Not one shoulder, but both shoulders. He put the sheep around his neck like a giant collar, and "wore" it all the way home. Then, obviously, the fifth movement is that the shepherd *carried it all the way home* (verse 6). "When (not *if*) he cometh home."

See if you can imagine the scene in your mind. The shepherd has found the sheep. Now, he follows the only procedure that will guarantee the sheep's recovery. He turns the sheep upside-down, bottom-side up, on its back. Thus, the four legs the sheep normally walks on are disqualified thereafter—all the way home! He encloses its two hind legs in one of his powerful hands, and its two front legs in his other powerful hand, picks it up, shifts its weight onto his strong body, swings it over his head, and places its full weight upon his shoulders, wearing it like a giant collar. Its

The Outrageous Love of God

head is beside one ear, and its tail beside the other. Do you see the picture? *Now, if the sheep gets off and gets away, whose fault is it? Why, it's the shepherd's fault!* It is perfectly guaranteed that if the sheep *could* get away, it would stray in time and get lost again. To prevent that, the shepherd follows the only saving procedure. If the shepherd follows any other course, the sheep only has *probation, not salvation.* But the shepherd's procedure secures full, complete, permanent salvation for the sheep.

Suddenly, that sheep has six legs! And the four it has normally walked on don't count any more! It will "walk" all the way home on the legs of Another! Now, my dear friend, if you believe you have a salvation which you can have today and lose at some time in the future, please don't offer your salvation to me. I have a salvation—the only kind God provides and Christ secures—which I can never lose. If I traded mine (His), a *perfect* salvation, for a *probated* salvation, what kind of foolish bargain would I be driving? I'm out of the wilderness, riding high on the Shepherd's shoulders, and headed for home! Wouldn't you like to join me?

His hands are big enough to hold all of us, and His shoulders powerful enough to carry all of us. Why occupy a lost position, exposed to every enemy, or a lesser position of insecurity, when Jesus' salvation "to the uttermost" (Hebrews 7:25) *is available to you?*

The Matter of the Mas
Missing Money

Luke 15:8-10

I. Created by Design

II. Corrupted by Dislocation

III. Continued in the Dwelling

IV. Concealed in Darkness

V. Covered with Dirt

VI. Caused a Disturbance

VII. A Center of Delight

e Matter of the Master's
Missing Money

Luke 15:8-10

Either what woman having ten pieces of silver, if she
lose one piece, doth not light a candle, and sweep the
house, and seek diligently till she find it? And when
she hath found it, she calleth her friends and neighbors
together, saying, Rejoice with me; for I have found the
piece which I had lost. Likewise, I say unto you, there is
joy in the presence of the angels of God over one sinner
that repenteth.

Note the comparisons between this part of the parable, the story
of a lost coin, and the preceding one, the story of the lost sheep.
Whereas in the first part of the story, it was a *male* shepherd
who suffered the loss of the sheep, in this part of the story, it is a
woman who suffers the loss and secures the recovery. Whereas in
the previous story, the loss suffered was *one* percent of the total
assets (one sheep out of a hundred), here the loss is *ten* percent
(one coin out of ten). Thus, we can easily see that the motive for
the recovery of the lost sheep was *pity* for the *object* that was
lost. Here, the motive is the *profit* of the *owner*. So Jesus is telling
us that both the lost person himself and God have a great stake
in the recovery of sinners, because both suffer intolerable losses
if individuals without God are not recovered. Observe, also, that
the sheep was lost *in a vast wilderness*, while the coin is lost *in*

The Outrageous Love of God

a small home. In the first case, one lone shepherd is matched against a vast wilderness to find one lost sheep; in the second case, one woman is matched against her small home to find one lost coin. So the second story appears to be considerably more hopeful than the first.

Another comparison is in the obvious *conditions* of the lost objects. I have said that a sheep, the lost object in the first part, is extremely *dumb*. But a coin is not even stupid—it's *dead!* So Jesus adds another stroke to produce a composite picture of what it means to be lost—not just dumb, drifting, and defenseless, but also dead. Is a lost person alive or dead? The answer is yes! He is psychologically and physically alive (alive in soul and body), but stone dead in his spirit, which is the only part of him that will finally count. Man is a trinity like God is, made of spirit, soul, and body (I Thess. 5:23). This order—spirit, soul, and body—is the order of eternal importance. But when Adam sinned, his spirit died instantly and totally. Incidentally, the spirit is the "compartment" within man for containing the Presence of God. When God made Adam, He made him with a healthy body, a happy soul, and a holy spirit (because it was indwelt by the Holy Spirit of God). But when Adam sinned, God departed out of Adam's spirit, and it instantly became a death chamber. Since that time, every person born of Adam (every human being except Jesus) has been born with a dead spirit. The Bible clearly says that men without God are "dead in trespasses and sins" (Ephesians 2:1). So this dead coin is an excellent picture of every person without Christ.

In this study, we will spotlight that dead drachma, that lost silver coin. I want you to see seven revealing facts about that coin, and note the parallels between the lost silver and the lost sinner.

I. Created by Design

First, that coin was created by design. It did not "just happen" to be a coin—by accident, or chance, or caprice. It was obviously created that way by specific intention. So man did not "just happen." He is not the product of a cosmic accident, whatever biased naturalistic scientists may tell us. When I was a boy, I was told the story of an ugly frog that was kissed by a beautiful maiden and became a handsome prince—and we called that a fairy story. Today, we hear of a frog becoming a man—and we call that "science!" Personally, *I still believe it to be a fantasy story!* It violates the first foundational premise of true science, which requires that the conclusions of science are drawn from, and based upon, the evidence at hand. Man, like the silver coin in the story, was created by design.

Note that this silver piece was a coin, not just a lump or a mass of silver. It was made in a certain way, with a certain appearance, and with a certain predetermined purpose and value. Its lines and markings are evident; it was clear-cut by the mint that made it. Obviously, man is not just a mass of substance. He is made in a certain way and with a certain predetermined structure, purpose and value.

Just as the coin bore a certain image and superscription, so does man. Jesus held a coin in His hand one day and asked

His audience, "Tell me, whose image and superscription does it bear?" His listeners replied, "Caesar's." So that coin was a "quiet advertisement" for the Roman Caesar anytime it was put to its normal use. One of the greatest questions of every age is to ask about man, "Whose image and superscription does he bear?" It is the clear statement of Scripture that man was created by God in His own image (Genesis 1:26-27). At out conception we were stamped or "minted" in the image of God. This means that we possess something in measure that God possesses in fullness.

We are like God in that we, too, are rational, moral, responsible, and self-transcending creatures, and we possess personal qualities that clearly distinguish us from animals. We can never dispense with the pattern of our creation without becoming terribly distorted and disrupted within ourselves, and this is precisely what has happened under the impact of atheistic humanism.

Suppose I hold in my hand a United States quarter, one-fourth of a dollar. Whose image is on it? That of George Washington. But where is George Washington? He certainly is not present when I hold the quarter in my hand. You see, in this case, the presence of the "original" (George Washington) is not required for the revealing of his image. The image is rather flat, lusterless, and limited, but it is still there. If I put the coin in my pocket, the image of "ol' George" is still on it. If I put it in an envelope and mail it halfway around the world, it still bears the image. If I take it 3,000 feet below the surface of the earth and leave it in the heart of a mine, the image will still be there. This is a rather crude illustration of the way every human being is made in the image of God. The relational Presence of the Great Original is not required for man's nature to be intact. Whether he is saved or lost, he is still indelibly imprinted with the image of God.

Suppose I hold in my hand a small mirror and hold it before my face. My face is reflected on the surface of the mirror. How long will the reflection be cast? As long as I hold the mirror before my face—and my face before the mirror. In this case, the presence of the "original" *is* required for the continuation of the reflection. This is a crude illustration of the manner in which a *saved* person "contains" and may reflect the image of God. When a sinner is saved, Jesus Christ, "the image of the invisible God" (Colossians 1:15), "the express image of God's person" (Hebrews 1:3), comes into that saved person. The entire Christian life thereafter is a relational development between Jesus and the saved sinner. The Presence of the Original remains without interruption in the believer, and thus he may "continue to reflect like a mirror the splendor of the Lord" (II Cor. 3:18, Williams translation).

Remember, also, that the coin in the story is silver. It is not a base metal, such as tin, or zinc, or iron, or lead. So the coin has a real, inherent value in itself, whether it is deployed in its intended use or displaced from that purpose. Don't forget this: every human being has a real, innate, inherent value in himself, even if he is totally missing the purpose of his existence. C. S. Lewis surely had this truth in his mind when he wrote,

"It is a serious thing to live in a society of possible gods and goddesses, to remember that the dullest and most uninteresting person you talk to may one day be a creature which, if you saw it now, you would be strongly tempted to worship, or else a horror and a corruption such as you now meet, if at all, only in a nightmare. All day long we are, in some degree, helping each other to one of the other of these destinations. It is in the light of these overwhelming possibilities, it is with the awe and the circumspection proper to them, that we should conduct all our dealings with one another, all friendships, all loves, all play, all politics. There are no *ordinary* people. You have never talked to a mere mortal. It is immortals whom we joke with, work with, marry, snub, and exploit—immortal horrors or everlasting splendors."

So every human being must live with the "high dignity" of handling his own inherent value. If he throws himself away and wastes that value, he is eternally accountable to the Manufacturer for the misuse. If he keeps himself in the ownership of the Great Treasurer, he is infinitely gratified in the fulfillment of his destiny.

This presents a question. What is a coin for, anyway? You see, if we want to know what anything is, a good way to find out is to ask what it is *for*. What is a butter knife? You could say it is a thin strip of steel, sharpened along one edge, and your statement would be accurate, though inadequate. If you said nothing more, you've said very little. If, on the other hand, you said that a butter knife is something you spread butter with, you'd be getting nearer the heart of the matter. So what is a coin for? A coin has two primary purposes. It is either to be *treasured* by its owner, or *traded* by its owner to obtain something of equal value to itself. What a picture of the purpose of our existence as human beings! God created us for these very purposes: to *treasure us unto Himself*, and/or *to trade us in as His "spending money" to "purchase" others of equal value to ourselves*. He wants to fully *possess* us, and to use us as *His purchasing power*, investing us in His interest on the world market to gain others like us for Himself. Could anything be clearer?

So we, like the coin in the story, were Created by Design.

II. Corrupted by Dislocation

Second, that coin was *corrupted by dislocation*. It became "lost" (vss. 8, 10) in the house. What does that mean? Well, it was still a coin, so its structure had not changed. It was still silver, so its nature had not changed. It was still valuable, so its worth had not changed. It was still marked, so its image had not changed. So why was it lost?

It was lost because it *fell* (!) *out of circulation*, and thus it was forfeited from its intended function. That coin was lost though it had *no consciousness or sensation* of being lost. It had *no discontent* or *anxiety* over being lost, but it was lost nonetheless. Here, Jesus is indicating to us that there are people who are more like *things* than *persons*. They have a *minimum of will*, and they allow their entire lives to be determined by circumstance rather than choice. They simply don't develop enough strength of character or force of will to resist the gravitation of a distracting or wicked or worldly environment.

So this part of the story adds this devastating "twist" to the picture of man's lostness. When a human being is lost, he is *worthless to God.* Perhaps I should reverse that to say, when a human being is *worthless to God,* he is *lost!* Romans 3:12, in one of the most terrible accounts of human lostness in all of Scripture (Romans 3:9-19), says, "They are all gone out of the way, they have together become *unprofitable.*" How much worth is accruing to God because of your daily lifestyle? How much dividend is God getting back from His creation of you? One of the greatest of Jesus' parables (Matthew 25:14-30) indicates that *there will be nobody in heaven who was useless to God on earth.*

Do you remember the English classic by Daniel DeFoe named *Robinson Crusoe*? It is a novel based on the true story of a shipwrecked sailor named Alexander Selkirk. In the novel, Robinson Crusoe is the sole survivor of a terrible shipwreck on the reefs of a deserted island. Crusoe was finally able to swim back out to the hull of the ship wrecked on the reef and salvage everything he felt might be useful to his survival. He salvaged some ropes, some bags of seeds, some farming tools, several kegs of gunpowder, several guns, and several large bags of gold and silver coins. He found a practical use for every other article he salvaged except the most "valuable" articles of all—the gold and silver coins! You see, on his island there was nothing to buy and nowhere to purchase. So the coins were "lost"—they were *out of circulation.*

Friends, we are the King's money, and He wants to possess us and use us. But a lost person, a person outside of Christ and His salvation, is *a blank in God's treasury. He is an empty spot in God's cash register.*

So we, like this coin, became Corrupted by Dislocation.

III. Continued in the Dwelling

Third, that coin *continued in the dwelling*, though it was lost. Though it was lost to its owner's possession and use, it still never got outside the house. If it, like the sheep, had been lost in the vast wilderness, the woman likely would not have wasted time or thought of effort on its recovery. If it had fallen into the Sea of Galilee, she might have mourned the loss, but she would have done nothing to recover it. But it was lost at home. Now remember, there are four lost things in this story, and two of them (the sheep and the prodigal son) are lost far, far away from safety, while the other two (the coin and the elder brother) are lost at home.

What is Jesus suggesting by these obvious realities? He is saying that a human being may be lost while in the near vicinity of the person and influence of his rightful owner. He may remain in the father's house for a long, long time, and still never know or be near his father's heart. It is possible for a person to be raised in a solidly Christian home, and be regularly "under the sound of chapel bell," in church and under Gospel influences, all of his life—and still be lost. You see, the truth is that the Devil would rather send you to hell from a church pew than a street gutter any day, because your presence in church falsely salves your conscience, falsely advertises a Christianity you don't really possess, and falsely protects you from the Savior by a regular inoculation of religion. Jesus once said to a man, "You are not far from the kingdom of God." Just like the coin and the elder brother, you may be very close to your owner and Savior, and still be lost. *You may have your hand on Heaven's doorknob and still go to Hell!* Beware of being lost in the house.

IV. Concealed in Darkness

Fourth, that coin was *concealed in darkness* inside the house. We know this because the woman had to light a lamp to find it (verse 8). A little background is necessary to understand this part of the story. The average Palestinian home of that day had only one room, and it was usually quite small. It often had a two-level floor, and the animals stayed on the "lower floor" in bad weather, while the family lived and slept on the upper level. The one door was quite small, often requiring a person to stoop to enter, and there often was only one window of perhaps twelve inches across—and it usually had a lattice across it. So there was very little natural light in the home even on the brightest day.

Consider the parallel between that situation and the condition of a lost sinner. The lost person does have a little natural light which points him to God, the light of creation and the light of conscience, "so that they are without excuse" (Romans 1:20; see Romans 1 and 2)—but this is not enough light to lead him to salvation. The light of Christ is necessary for that! Jesus said, "I am the light of the world; he who follows after me shall not walk in darkness, but shall have the light of life" (John 8:12). The saving light is "the light of the knowledge of the glory of God in the face of Jesus Christ" (II Corinthians 4:6). Without that light, the lost person remains in the dark. Psalm 107:10 says that he "sits in darkness and in the shadow of death." When God saves him, he transfers him "out of darkness into His marvelous light" (I Peter 2:9). Meanwhile, as a lost sinner, he remains concealed in darkness.

V. Covered with Dirt

Fifth, that coin was *covered with dirt* inside the house. We know this because verse eight says that she "swept (a strong word: 'scoured') the house." Again, a bit of background would help us here. The floor of the typical Palestinian home of that day was a dirt floor. To protect from the dust, the owner often covered the floor with a mat of dried reeds or rushes. It is then very easy to reconstruct the scene in Jesus' story. The coin slipped unseen out of its place in the owner's possession, and undoubtedly had settled down into a place among those reeds or rushes so that it could not be detected by the eye. So she had to sweep the house in order to find and repossess it. Even so, lost men, while still bearing the image of God, is covered by the dirt of his own depravity, and thus the image is not easily detectable. It may be so covered, so marred, so defaced, that his is like an old broken down temple whose past glory is only guessed at by viewing its present ruins.

When I was a boy, I lived with my parents only half a city block away from the railroad track that ran through the heart of our town. Many times I placed a coin on that railroad track when the train was approaching, left it there while the train passed over it, and then recovered it when the train was gone. Sometimes the residue was only an enlarged, thin, flat, shiny piece of silver, completely unrecognizable when compared to the coin it had been. If the train was a long one, or a loaded one, the coin would be so thin that it could now be easily bent further out of shape. I thought of those memories when I read this story. Sin flattens out the sinner, and then, easily bends him further out of shape. It sometimes would take a "lucky guess" to surmise that some men are made in the likeness of God. The image has been so badly distorted and impaired that it would take a sharp investigator to see the vestige of it that remains, but it is still there. The individual is still convertible though covered with dirt.

VI. Caused a Disturbance

That coin, though lost, concealed in darkness, and covered with dirt, *caused a big disturbance* inside the house. When the woman discovered her loss, her sense of loss created a dreadful disturbance inside that house. Did you know that your only hope of salvation is in God's sense of deprivation over your lostness? You simply cannot save yourself—any more than that coin could restore itself to its owner's hand—and your hope for restoration is in the frustration and despair of the owner over losing you.

Give special attention to *the woman who was disturbed* in this story. Remember that the owner of the lost object in this part of the story was a housewife. She is the only *woman* who appears in the total chapter. The shepherd (verses 3-7) was a male. The two sons (verses 11-32) were, of course, males. And the father was a male. Why is the owner and searcher in this part of the parable a female? Who does this woman represent?

In the account of the lost sheep, the shepherd obviously represents Jesus, who called Himself "the Good Shepherd." In the account of the prodigal son and the elder brother, the father obviously represents God the Father. Nothing could be easier and clearer than these identifications. But what about this woman? Well, if the shepherd represents Jesus the Son of God, and the father represents God the Father, whom would you guess this woman would represent? That's correct. The Holy Spirit! The Holy Spirit personally plays something of a female role in the Godhead, and is often pictured in the Bible in feminine terms. In Genesis chapter one, the text says that "the Spirit of God brooded over the face of the deep." The picture is that of a female bird hovering over a nest of eggs to bring baby birds to birth. The picture in Genesis one is that of the Spirit hovering over a chaotic universe to bring a new creation to birth. It is a female picture. The Holy Spirit does a courting and wooing work in the hearts of men to establish a love relationship between them and God. In fact, so pronounced in this work in the Bible that Norman Harrison wrote a book entitled *The Mothering Ministry of the Holy*. But there is something else apparently intended in this part of Jesus' parable. The woman represents the Holy Spirit working in and through another entity which is pictured in the New Testament in female terms. The Church of Jesus Christ is pictured as the Bride of Christ. It will finally be presented to Him as a perfect bride, "without wrinkle and without spot." So the woman in this account represents the Holy Spirit of God acting in and through the Church, the Bride of Christ.

Give careful attention to *the work this woman did* in the story. The work she did was in four separate acts, and each is highly significant in understanding the Holy Spirit's work in bringing lost sinners to God.

First, she *shined a light*. Verse eight says, "She lit a lamp" (the word is "lamp" rather than "candle," as the King James Version says). What does this represent? By the hermeneutical principle of "the analogy of Scripture," the Bible interprets itself. It says in Psalm 119:105, "Thy Word is a lamp unto my feet, and a light unto my path." This lamp represents the Bible, the Word of God, which is the first and greatest instrument the Holy Spirit uses in bringing lost people to salvation. But do not take anything for granted! It is not the presence (or preaching) of the Bible that brings people unto God. *The lamp was effective in the story only when it was lit.* The Bible must be illumined to the human heart by a miracle of the Holy Spirit—*the lighting of the lamp!* If the Bible is preached without the powerful anointing of the Spirit upon it (without the lamp being lit), it becomes "the letter of the law," and it only advances men in spiritual death. So the most important activity inside the house is for members of the household to ask God to "light the lamp"! Jesus said, "My house shall be called the House of Prayer." Never should the Church be in assembly without the members of God's family praying earnestly, *"Oh, God, light the lamp!"* When the lamp is lit, the Holy Spirit has begun His great searching crusade—inside the house.

Second, she *swept the house*. One commentator points out the strength of the word translated "sweep" in the text by saying that it literally means to "clean by scouring." This woman conducted a crusade inside the house that day. She held a campaign! She turned everything upside down in her search for the lost coin. She sent clouds of dust into the air all over the house that day. How would you like to have been a family member at home that day? You would probably have alternated between coughs and protests all day long. Remember, the typical home of that day was a small one-room building. She could not sweep the house without disturbing and disrupting everything and everybody. Friends, when the Holy Spirit lights the lamp and begins to scour the house, the status quo is immediately terribly disturbed. But as one African-American pastor put it, "Our status ain't nothin' to *quo about*, anyway!" Many of us will fight to preserve the death inside the house, but if we knew what would happen when the Holy Spirit lights the lamp, turns the house upside down, and finds the lost, we would happily give up the usual mediocrity that prevails among us.

Third, she *secured the coin*. She satisfied the quest of her own heart and restored the coin to its proper place. "She found it," Jesus said. It was now back in her possession, to be treasured by her or traded by her, as she wished. Translate this part of the story into the action of Heaven, and imagine the heart of God as He finds that which was lost.

Fourth, she *shared a celebration*. "And when she hath found it, she calleth her friends and her neighbors together, saying, Rejoice with me; for I have found the piece which I had lost." Then Jesus "edited" the earthly story with Heaven's addition: "Likewise, I say unto you, there is joy in the presence of the angels of God over one sinner that repenteth." Every part of the story in which a lost thing was found ends with a *party*.

That lost coin became the focal point of a giant disturbance in that house that day. Everything was turned upside down in order for that woman to find the coin. But the disturbance was worth it, even if the other members of the household didn't realize it. Friends, nobody is ever saved without a giant disturbance! There will be a disturbance *within* and *without*. The lost person will feel himself tossed about in the Spirit's crusade to save him, and the entire household will feel the distress. And some family members may be upset by the disturbance! But thank God, He doesn't wait to please every member of the household before He saves the lost.

VII. A Center of Delight

Finally, the coin in that story became an absolute *center of delight*. The woman called a neighborhood party which included all of her friends. And Jesus said that this was only a tiny picture of what happens in Heaven when one sinner is drawn out of the darkness, dirt, and death of sin and brought home to God.

Give careful heed to the fact that *Jesus knows what makes God happy!* And the fact that Jesus was perfectly familiar with what was occurring in Heaven while He was standing solidly in a human body right here on earth! And He points out the goals of Heaven to us.

A Presbyterian mother was rehearsing her little daughter in the Shorter Catechism. She quoted the first question to her: "What is the chief end of man?" The little girl recited the answer: "The chief end of man is to glorify God, and to enjoy Him forever." The mother idly asked, "Then what is the chief end of *God?*" The little girl had not thought of *this* question, but she quickly guessed an answer. "Mommy, if the chief end of *man* is to glorify God and to enjoy Him forever, then the *chief end of God must be to glorify **man** and to **enjoy him forever**.*" If her answer was a guess, it was an inspired guess! **God is gratified when man is glorified!**

The Bible calls God "the blessed God," but the word "blessed" doesn't do justice to the word. The word is actually "happy." He is "the *happy* God." But the text tells that there is something we can do to enhance His happiness. We are forever asking God to do things for us that will make us happy. Look at the story one final time and ask yourself, What could I do today to *make* **God** *happy?*

The Long Way Home

Luke 15:11-24

I. "I Want My Share"

    A. Proper desire—the first step in selfhood

    B. Perverted desire—the first stains of selfishness

II. "I Want My Way"

    A. Majored on the "bondage" of the household

    B. Minored on the "blessings" of the household

    C. Moved to the "freedom" of the far country

III. "I Want"

    A. The blight of waste

    B. The beginning of wisdom

IV. "I am Wanted"

    A. Not worthy, but wanted

    B. Not as a servant, but as a son

V. "I Shall Not Want"

    A. For forgiveness

    B. For fellowship

    C. For food

    E. For fullness of life

    F. For a future

The Long Way Home

Luke 15:11-24

And Jesus said, A certain man had two sons: And the younger of them said to his father, Father, give me the portion of goods that falleth to me. And he divided unto them his living. And not many days after the younger son gathered all together, and took his journey into a far country, and there wasted his substance with riotous living. And when he had spent all, there arose a mighty famine in that land; and he began to be in want. And he went and joined himself to a citizen of that country; and he sent him into his fields to feed swine. And he would fain have filled his belly with the husks that the swine did eat: and no man gave unto him. And when he came to himself, he said, How many hired servants of my father's have bread enough and to spare, and I perish with hunger! I will arise and go to my father, and will say unto him, Father, I have sinned against heaven, and before thee, And am no more worthy to be called thy son: make me as one of thy hired servants. And he arose, and came to his father. But when he was yet a great way off, his father saw him, and had compassion, and ran, and fell on his neck, and kissed him. And the son said unto him, Father, I have sinned against heaven, and in thy sight, and am no more worthy to be called thy son. But the father said to his servants, Bring forth

The Outrageous Love of God

the best robe, and put it on him; and put a ring on his hand, and shoes on his feet: And bring hither the fatted calf, and kill it; and let us eat, and be merry. For this my son was dead, and is alive again; he was lost, and is found. And they began to be merry.

One day, G.K. Chesterton, the great London journalist and spokesman for Christ, was packing his bags in his London apartment when a friend happened by. When he found Chesterton packing travel bags, he inquired idly, "Are you taking a trip?" Chesterton replied wryly, "Yes, I'm taking a trip *to London*." "But you're *already in London*," protested the surprised friend, "how can you be *going* to London?" Chesterton's answer revealed his usual wise insight and penetrating perception. He replied, "Oh, no, my friend, that's where you're wrong. I no longer *see London*, though I live in it. Familiarity has closed my eyes to it. The real meaning of travel is to go away from home so that when you come back, it is as if you saw it for the very first time. So I am going to London—by way of Paris, and Dresden, and Frankfort, and Rome."

The St. Louis writer, T. S. Eliot, in a play called *Little Gidding*, echoed Chesterton's sentiments when he said,

We shall not cease from exploration.

And the end of all our exploring

Will be to arrive where we started

And know the place for the first time.

In "the greatest short story ever told," Jesus' parable of the prodigal son, there is a perfect illustration of the sayings of both Chesterton and Eliot. This is the immortal story of a young man who "took the long way home." The young man in the story was brought to great extremity *away from home* so that he might come back and *see* his home and his father *for the very first time*. In this study, we will trace the dispositional and philosophical steps he took in making the long journey home—by way of a far country.

I. "I Want My Share"

The first step in the journey taken by the young man in Jesus' story could be labeled, *"I want my share."* The young man said to his father, "Father, give me the portion of goods that falleth to me." On the surface, it seems like such a natural request. Ambitious, but natural. The boy asked for no more than his due—"the portion of goods that falleth to me," the inheritance he was due to receive as the younger son in his father's family. He only wanted what his father had already reserved for him.

It is hard to fault the young man for wanting what was only his birthright, his *right by birth*. Any student of life knows that the awakening of *want* is a time of great importance in any life. That awakening is an indispensable requirement for our personal fulfilment. The awareness of a new or deep want often may be the clearest evidence of God's dealings with us. In fact, need and desire are our two leading tickets of admission to God's Treasure House. You see, God's provisions are made prior to our

The Outrageous Love of God

awareness of need of them and our asking for them. There are resources and reserves in the economy of God that wait for our praying. The first Christians realized that God had provided a fabulous inventory of blessings—love, joy, peace, and a multitude of other blessings of many kinds and sizes. And *we today* may be sure that such gifts have never been withdrawn. God has a vast inheritance of riches which rightfully belong to His child (Ephesians 1:11). So any request for "my share" looks innocent enough on the surface. In fact, a person will never come to his full inheritance unless he wants his share.

However, when we look a bit deeper into the circumstantial, domestic and cultural background, we see dark clouds beginning to form by means of this boy's request of his father. You see, the inheritance laws said that the estate was divided upon the death of its owner. In this case, it was the father's estate that was in question. So the boy already showed an insensitive lack of concern for anyone in his home circle. In effect, *he was willing to wish for the death of his father* so that he might have his share. The first deep stains of selfishness showed through the thin garment of his family respectability when he made the request, "I want my share." However, it must be realized that this very request also brings to the surface his best chance to be saved. After all, he would have never come back home at the end of his long journey if he had not realized there was a share left for him at home, even if it was reduced (as he thought) by his delinquency.

Let me simply say that *all selfish requests in life made by sinful human beings* (all human beings) *have inherent in them an attack upon the life of the God who owns the estate. Sin contains a hidden "death-wish" directed at God. This is the meaning of the Cross. Man as a sinner had his way with a holy God, and it mean death to Him.* So we must be very, very careful when we say, "I want my share," careful that our desire and request are on legitimate and holy grounds. If the request is made wrongly, we have taken the first step to the poverty of the far country. Let's see how it developed in the remainder of the story.

II. "I Want My Way"

The second step in the boy's journey began when he followed the request for his share with another request, *"I want my **way**."* "And not many days after the younger son gathered all together, and took his journey into a far country." Apparently the boy thought that the rules, regulations, and restraints of his father's home were violating his desire for a free and satisfying life. As is typical in the many such cases we know about, he probably began to major on negatives, restraints, prohibitions, laws, rules, and regulations. Like most people who never think deeply enough about life, he failed to see that there is more freedom in negative restrictions than there is in positive commands. If I say, *"Don't* stand *there,"* I have allowed you the freedom to be absolutely anywhere else. But if I say, "Stand *there,"* I have reduced your freedom to one tiny spot. It was easier for this boy to press for his own selfish satisfaction than to think about distant consequences. He magnified the threats to his "freedom," and began to mistrust and misunderstand his father.

The young man *formed a wrong opinion about his father*, and had *a false conceit about himself*—the invariable story of all sin. The sinner is unteachable and unreachable at this point. Satan obliges him by giving him a selfish stubbornness that matches his own. Of course, the sinner himself always "knows better" than the experience, wisdom, and testimony "of the ages." Of course, his story is unique, his life is exceptional, his desires are "God-given," and he will "beat the rap." The naivete of this course is incredible, but every new generation has millions who swallow Satan's bait, "hook, line and sinker." The father who waits heart-brokenly at home must only hope that the journey to the far country doesn't exact the ultimate toll—health, sanity, resources, even life itself. But the risk of the prodigal is that many find the end of the trail in the far country—and then regret forever that they didn't look more closely at the real nature of the father's heart and home.

One of Aesop's famous fables concerns the old lion and the fox. The lion was getting too hold to hunt. He said, "I've got to eat, but I'm too old to hunt. So I will spread the word that I'm sick and my friends will come to see me." So he did, and all the animals came and, of course, he would grab them and devour them. An easy way both to hunt and to live. The fox came over to see the lion one day saying, "Yoo Hoo, Mr. Lion." And the lion answered, "Yoo Hoo, Mr. Fox. Come in and see me. I'm sick and tired." Mr. Fox said, "I believe I'll just visit you through the window." "Oh, do come in," said Mr. Lion. Mr. Fox said, "No, I'll just visit from outside." The lion asked, "Mr. Fox, why won't you come in?" The fox answered, "Mr. Lion, I have been studying the tracks. They all lead in and none lead out." This is the tragic truth of the far country. The happy ending of Jesus' story is an exceptional victory of grace. All the tracks lead into the far country—but few lead out!

A young man with the gleam of the lights of the far country in his eye and raging selfish tastes in his heart never realizes the price of this selfish lifestyle. The Bible says of all men that "all we like sheep have gone astray, we have turned every one to his own way" (Isaiah 53:6)—and that is God's definition of sin. "We have turned every one *to his own way*." "I want my way" is the life-motto of the man without God. While the way of pardon, purpose, peace and power, the Perfect Way, is found only in a happy relationship with the Father, the sinner totally disregards this Way in the claim that he knows better than anybody else what he wants and needs. The Bible answers, "The heart is deceitful above all things, and desperately wicked; who can know it?" (Jeremiah 17:9).

This young man "took his journey into a far country." The far country is any place where a human being attempts to live without God. It can be a position on a church pew, a place in a respectable home, an executive's spot in a great company—any place where a human being lives without a vital relationship with God.

The boy had rationalized (the usual course of stubborn sinners), "I just want to call my own signals. After all, *I'm* on the playing field. The coach on the sidelines doesn't know what will work for me." "I want to have my own fling." "I have natural desires. What could possibly be wrong with satisfying them?" "I want to be a free man." "I want to follow nature." *"I can manage my own life better than he (He) can!"* The sinner has not learned yet that this universal law is never broken: *To be self-managed is to be self-damaged. To run your own life is to ruin your own life.* I repeat: this law is never broken—but many a selfish and rebellious person *has broken himself on it.* No one ever really breaks the law of God, but every violator of it is broken by it. A "wise" sinner is one who sees his sins as God sees them and is broken before God as a violator of the law. A "wilful, stupid" sinner is one who clings to his sins as if he were the captain of his fate and the master of his soul. Dear friend, do not forget that the count is not final until God casts His vote! If you are near His heart and "at home" where He is, His vote is a thumbs-up approval. But if you have faced away from Him and His Standard and have wilfully assumed your own course, whatever God and His Word may say, the mud of the pigsty in the far country is like cement and the corn husks of the final diet there are desperately dry (to say nothing of the other losses that often attend that course).

SIN is *Self -Ish - Ness*

Sin is *Autonomy*, or "Self-law"

Sin is *private purposing*

Sin is *doing without God*

Sin is *going it alone*

There are only two philosophies on life's shelf,

Either live for Christ or live for self.

Two prayers divide men. Every person is living by one of these two prayers at this very moment. One is the prayer of Jesus, "Not my will, but Thine be done." The other is the prayer of Satan, "Not Thy will, *but mine* be done." If you exercise faith in Jesus Christ, the holy and perfect Son of God, you pray with Him, "Not my will, but Thine be done," and you go with Him where He is. But if you maintain self-government against all the loving overtures of God, you pray with Satan, "Not Thy will, but mine be done," and you go with him where he is. If you want to see the result of "My will be done," follow the revealed course of Satan in the Bible, all the way to his dispatch into the Lake of Fire. If you want to see the result of "Thy will be done," follow the revealed course of Jesus in the Bible, all the way through the Cross to His super-exaltation above all things.

But the boy left home, convinced that he could prove that there is plenty of fun in the far country. After all, would sin have any appeal if there were no fun or self-gratification in it? However, to depart from the will of God is to depart from freedom into slavery. Two things are always in the course of spiritual independence: *waste* (Luke 15:13) and *want* (Luke 15:14). So the next movement of the story is quite predictable.

III. "I Want"

The third movement of the story is as abrupt as the price of sin, *"I want."* We may be sure that the boy's first fling at the far country produced a heady period of exciting enchantment. But the dregs are not far off when the first sip of sin is swallowed. So the story truthfully traces the outer arc of "the long way home" by saying, "And there (in the far country) he wasted his substance with riotous living" (Luke 15:13). Another translation puts it even more vividly, "He squandered his resources in loose living." And verse fourteen graphically adds, "And he began to be *in want.*"

The farthest reach of the far country may be traced in seven sad sentences in the text:

(1) "He wasted his substance with riotous living." Waste means that there was a steady disbursement of possessions, but without any adequate return. But notice the phrase, *"His* substance." Whose? Who did the resources *really* belong to? What was their *real* source? The boy had not earned them. He had not amassed the wealth he was now spending. He was a parasite on somebody else's resources. The possessions he spent so easily were not the product of his own hand. You have seen the bumper sticker that says, "We are spending our children's inheritance." Well, this boy was spending his *father's* endowment. *"His* substance," the substance that had been given him (probably reluctantly) upon request by his father. Dear friend, do you know what this means? It means that *God* sponsors the prodigal's trip into the far country! It means that *God* finances the sinner's trip! Now, before you act too negatively to that idea,

think it through. After all, no sinner has a single resource that has not been given to him by God. When he shakes his fist in God's face, he uses a fist that God gave him through creation and birth. When he blasphemes God with a vagrant tongue, he can only use the tongue God gave to him. When he sets his feet to make the trip to the far country, he uses feet that God has given to him. His entire endowment of resources came from God! And he turns around and uses them to break God's heart, blaspheme God's Name, disbelieve God's Word, and crucify God's Son! "He wasted his substance in riotous living."

(2) "He spent all." There is only *expenditure*, never *investment*, in the far country. There is no dividend in the far country. The agenda of the far country calls for disbursement of goods with no adequate return. The inevitable outcome of waste is that the available resources are soon spent, and there is no means of replenishment in the far country.

(3) "There arose a mighty famine." Be careful to see this line. Be careful to examine this truth. Any insurance company labels a famine as "An Act of God." One of the Old Testament prophets called a famine "God's chosen fast." Hear this with great care. Trace the famines in Scripture and you will see that God went after many of His prodigal children with famines. He used a whale to fetch Jonah and a rooster to call Simon Peter back from the far country, and many other means with others of His own, but He often put His people on a "starvation diet" by sending a famine (read the story of God's child, Naomi, in the book of Ruth). Dear friend, you may inscribe this in stone:

If you are in a far country of sin, and a rooster, whale, or famine does not begin to come to where you are, *you are no child
of God!* In that case, the far country may not bother you. You
may enjoy the bright lights, the warm bodies that snuggle up
close for a little extra-curricular "love," and the companionship
of unhindered individuals. But no rooster will crow, no whale
will open its jaws, no famine will come to push you back home.
Oh, no, but *Hell will* open *its* jaws, and a diet of dusty death will
be yours *forever!* And may God forgive me if I say these things
with the spirit of the elder brother in the story, and not the spirit
of the broken-hearted Father! In fact, I have *been* God's prodigal
son many times! But the appeal still holds: Why put up with a
famine in a miserable far country when you can be close to an
all-providing Father?

(4) "He began to be in want." You see, the far country has
no currency of its own. The only wage it pays is death (Romans
6:23). The first gleam of hope for this boy's recovery is that "he
began to be in want," but this happens while he is still on the
downward path. This seems to be enough of a plunge to startle
a thinking person into reality, but *he hasn't reached bottom yet.*
He even tried to deny his want, but he was only prolonging his
rebellion.

(5) "He went and joined himself to a citizen of that country;
and he sent him into his fields to feed swine." This is the *freedom*
he wanted! This was the life without regulations he was seeking
when he left home! The verb "joined" is in the passive voice,
which means that he was at the mercy of the judgment of the

far country and could not help himself. Satan entices you with glamor and glitter, and then turns off all the lights to leave you in gloom. Satan uses you up, and then throws you away. This boy went for the beautiful faces and warm bodies of the far country, but now he has been digested by the far country, and is in its bowels! Here is a proud *Jewish* young man, formerly living off of the bounty of a wealthy father, now lifting each foot to the sound of sucking mud in a *pig* sty.

Several men were having a beer party in the woods. All of a sudden, there came a downpour of rain accompanied by crashing thunder. Two of the men ran for several minutes in the pouring rain, and finally reached their car just as the rain let up. They jumped in the car, started it up and headed down the road, laughing and, of course, resuming their beer drinking.

All of a sudden an old man's face appeared in the passenger window and tapped lightly on the window. The passenger screamed in terror, "Do you see that? It's a man's face at the window. It has to be a ghost!" The driver tried to maintain composure. He said, "Well, open the window a crack and see what he wants!" So the passenger rolled his window down a few inches and called out in a breaking voice, "What do you want?" The old man softly replied, "Do you have any tobacco?" "Tobacco," said the passenger, "he wants tobacco!" "Well, offer him a cigarette, and HURRY!" said the driver. So the passenger jerked out his cigarette pack and handed the old man a cigarette. Then he yelled, "Step on it! Let's get out of here!" The driver floor-boarded the gas pedal and watched the speedometer climb all the way up to 65 miles an hour. The two men looked at each other and the driver said, "How could that be? I was driving pretty fast."

Suddenly, the old man's face appeared at the window again. In panic, the passenger rolled down his window a little and asked, "What do you want now?" "Do you have a light?" the old man asked. The driver opened his window and threw a lighter over the top of the car. He grabbed a beer can, took a drink, and pushed the speed of the car up faster.

All of a sudden, the man's face appeared at the window again, and he knocked on the glass. The passenger rolled down the window and shouted, "WHAT DO YOU WANT?" The old man quietly answered, *"Would you like some help getting out of the mud?"*

While drinking the heady wine of the far country, the storm is liable to strike at any time. But when it does, the intoxicated prodigal may not know yet the full seriousness of his situation. He may still think he can "step on the gas" and make it on his own, but all the while he is only miring himself more deeply, not just in mud, but in the most distasteful and disgraceful mud of all, the mud of the pigsty.

Remind yourself that this story was directed by Jesus to *Jews*, to Jewish *rulers*, to Jewish *scribes*, and to *Pharisees*. Do you know what "swine" were to *them*? The ultimate in embarrassment, in disgrace, in humiliation, in degradation! Though they were upstanding citizens in the religious establishment in Jerusalem, and regular adherents in the Temple of God, their pride and self-righteousness put them in the degradation of the far country.

This boy did not leave home to become the world's worst sinner. On the contrary, he left with the idea, "Don't worry about me. I'll be OK." He would have hotly denied the possibility of a "hog pen ending." "That won't happen to me." He thought, as all excited sinners do, that he could play with fire and not get burned; he was going to "eat his cake and have it too." This is a big part of the illusion, the deceitfulness of sin.

(6) "He would fain have filled his belly with the husks that the swine did eat." The word "husks" is literally "pods." A few days before he was throwing his riches around as if they would last forever, but the run on resources in the far country soon empties the bank account. A boy whose tastes were conditioned to wining and dining suddenly found his teeth closing on a food that tasted like dry parchment. But he was so reduced that he was glad to get that. He is getting closer every minute to seeing the Face-at-Home, to hearing the Voice-from-Home!

(7) "And no man gave unto him." I repeat: the far country has no currency of its own. People who have come to the far country were selfish to begin with, and their selfishness is compounded by the fact that others around them cannot minister to them when their resources are gone. Furthermore, nobody cares in the far country. The rule is, "Each for himself, and the devil take the hindmost." As the devil picks them off, everybody seems to be hurrying toward the end of the line. When a poor sinner stubbornly holds to a course of sin, thinking that his action is *not* sin, and that even if it is, *his case is exceptional,*

he finally learns the hard way that *the Devil is a liar and always plays for keeps.*

The far country has nothing to give and no one to care. The boy had reached the end of his rope, the end of his resources, and the *end of himself.* "He came to himself," Jesus said. Where, then, had he been? He had been outside himself, at least! Here Jesus tells us the very history of sin. If he "came to himself," he had been *beside himself,* or *beneath himself.* Beside himself!? What does that mean? It is the very term we use for *insanity*! This boy had been acting as if he were mentally deranged. Do you realize that there is only one letter's difference between "insanity" and "insinity"? To be *in sin* is to be *insane.* When the veils of thoughtlessness are pulled aside, this is easy to see. Sin is a declaration of independence from God, but it is "in Him that we live, and move, and have our being." Is it sensible to declare independence from our very life Source? No, it is insane!

Think of the proposition a man *accepts* to remain in sin. "You are smart enough to color outside the lines without reprisal, without penalty. You are above the need for rules and regulations. You don't need Divine love; there is plenty of *free* love floating around in this world, and all I have to do is make myself available. Depend on God? No, thank you. I'll leave that course for weaklings who can't stand alone."

Worse, think of the proposition a man must *reject* to remain in sin. The world abounds with overtures and invitations from Heaven's loving God. God's Book makes a clear offer of amnesty to every sinner, plus many invitations to receive God's Gift of

Eternal Life. And the sinner clings instead to His "independence"! He deliberately walks away from the God in Whose hand his life is held. His lifestyle continually rebuts God's authority and rebuffs God's advances. Such a course is indeed insane.

Every single sin comprises a combination of *suicide* (self-murder), *homicide* (other-murder), and *Deicide* (God-murder). No wonder the Bible promises extreme penalties against sin! The Bible says that "the hearts of the sons of men is full of evil, and *madness is in their heart while they live*" (Ecclesiastes 9:3).

When he realized he was in want and couldn't get out, "he came to himself, and said, How many hired servants of my father's have bread enough and to spare, and I (emphatic, 'yes, *I*') perish with hunger! I will arise and go to my father, and will say unto him, Father, I have sinned against heaven, and before thee, And am no more worthy to be called thy son: make me as one of thy hired servants. And he arose, and came to his father." Now, the distance between himself and his father's house and heart is getting shorter with each step that he takes. And what a discovery he makes when he nears his father's house!

IV. "I am Wanted"

"He arose, and came to his father." As the desperate prodigal boy neared his old home, he made this startling discovery: *"I am wanted!"* Be sure to catch the dimensions of the story as his homegoing developed. Luke 15:17 says, "And when he came to himself, he said, How many hired servants of my father's have bread enough to spare, and I perish with hunger!" "Hired scrvants" are not even as high as slaves! This boy is now seeing the high privileges of the *lowest* residents at home! How his perspective has changed! The "hired hands" of my father's house are "surrounded with loaves" (the actual words he used), "but," "*but*," "I am perishing out here with hunger." I am pinching myself. What in the world am I doing out here? How did I ever allow myself to get to this place? How could I have ever been so *stupid*? That's it! What stupid steps I have taken, while thinking I was so smart. I wouldn't listen to anybody, and see where it has gotten me! Hobnobbing with the hogs! Mully-grubbing in the mud! Is this really me? So the text says, "He came to himself" (verse 17) . . . and then "he came to his father" (verse 20).

However, on the way home, he almost made another "far country" mistake. In his home-going resolution, he recited what he thought was an appropriate prayer: "Father, I have sinned against heaven (note his new realism; 'my sins have been an assault on God!'), and before thee, and am no more worthy to be called your son: make me as one of thy hired servants." I want to be very careful here, but I think he almost reverted back to a subtle "dictation mentality," the same kind of mentality that dominated him when he left home. Beginning at the words, "Make me," he may assumed an authoritative stance again. And he may have subtly thought, "My father will surely be impressed with my need, my humility, my begging, and show me mercy!"

You see, dear heart, when you have defaulted into the far country, and have been awakened to see the treasonous nature of your sins, all terms for returning to Your Father's House are taken out of your hands. The hardest thing on earth to honestly say is, "I have sinned." Check it in the Bible, and you will find that most of the times individuals said it, they were masking their continuing rebellion under patronizing piety. The flesh argues for its own virtue even while it is framing its confession of sin! Do not trust even your own sorrow over sin, or your "repentance." II Corinthians 7:10 says there is a "sorrow of the world which leads to death." This is the sorrow of getting caught, the sorrow of embarrassing yourself with your own stupidity, the sorrow of suffering deprivation in the far country. But there is a "godly sorrow that leads to repentance not to be repented of." It is this "unrepentable repentance" that we must have, and it is a gift of God as we look solely and exclusively to Him.

The flesh subtly tries to *purchase* the father's favor by its "lowliness" and "humility." This, I think, is the reason the father would not let the boy complete the confession when he arrived home (verses 21 and 22). He placed his hand on the boy's lips and cut off the possibility of dictation. "I will accept your broken will; don't even risk the subtle danger of misrepresenting the case." How gracious God is! He knows the lurking potential of our twisted flesh even when we are praying, even when we are worshiping, even when we are confessing sin—yes, *even when we are returning from the far country*. So the father's love and mercy combined to stop the confession at its mid-point. God's love is almost impatient to act! God's mercy will cover more sin than we realize! So the father sealed the boy's lips and got to the happy business of restoration.

The Outrageous Love of God

Rehearse the homecoming again. The boy is now heading home. "When he was yet a great way off, his father saw him, and had compassion, and ran, and fell on his neck, and kissed him." You see, the boy had been far away from his father's home, but he was never out of his father's heart. Every day, the father went up on the housetop and fitted the telescope of love to his eye of compassion and scanned the horizon, hoping for the best. "The father saw him." When the lens of the father's telescope of love drew the son's image into focus, a sudden succession of restoring actions was set in motion. "The father had compassion." The word "compassion" is the Greek word for the intestines of one's body. It is often translated "the bowels of compassion." When this man saw his son on the road of return, his visceral area heaved up as if churning within him. This is "gutsy" grace! Remember, this is a picture of God—*painted by the One who knows Him best, His own Beloved Son!*

"He had compassion, *and ran.*" The father ran to his son! The vagrant son limped toward the homestead, and the father ran to meet him! The father runs to welcome him, though the prodigal walks home. In verse 13, when the boy "took his journey into a far country," the aorist tense is used. His journey, though it was a long one, is pictured in the text as a kind of quantum leap. He was so eager to get there that his journey was hurried, like a single step. Here, when the father runs, the same verb tense is used, the aorist tense. He ran at such a speed that it was like one sudden step. Friends, *this is the only time in the Bible (!) God is ever pictured as running! The Father gets in a big hurry when*

He is moving to welcome a refugee back from the far country of sin! How could this boy miss seeing how *wanted* he was at home? How can sinners fail to see how much the Father wants them home? Dear friend, the lights are on in your room, and the Father waits at the gate—He wants you, yes, *you*, home!

> God loves you more than you can ever know,
> And once the long trip home is begun,
> He will rush to greet you on your way.
> He will run! Yes, God will even run!

Another poet made it even more personal:

> The fatted calf, the robe, the shoes, the ring,
> They are all for me, though I am an unworthy son,
> But the most wonderful thing is that God ran to meet me,
> Yes, *I saw God run.*

Some years ago, I heard a sermon on Zacchaeus, the little Jewish tax collector who met Jesus at the foot of a sycamore tree on a city tree in the city of Jericho. I don't remember anything about the sermon, but I wrote down the simple outline. The sermon was preached from the viewpoint of Zacchaeus himself, and the points were:

I. He *sees* me.
II. He *knows* me.
III. He *loves* me.
IV. He *wants* me.
V. He *can have me.*

The Outrageous Love of God

The prodigal boy made the same kind of incredible discovery out on the road just short of his father's house. His heart must have fairly sung with relief, hope, and joy. "I am actually wanted by my father!"

V. "I Shall Not Want"

Then he came to one last happy discovery: *"I shall not want."* The boy was embraced in his father's arms, smothered by his father's kisses, silenced by his father's grace, and endowed with his father's possessions.

He discovered that day that he would not "want" or lack anything that was necessary for his true happiness. "I shall not want" for *my father's forgiveness*. He had honestly confessed, "Father, I have sinned against heaven and in your sight, and I am not worthy to be called your son," and when the father heard that humble confession, he made a full grant of his forgiveness to the repenting son. And it is a significant feature in Jesus' parable to note that *the boy never speaks again in the remainder of the account*. Apparently, he had come to a full realization of his sins, and thus he was able to come to a full appreciation of his father's forgiveness. And it left him speechless! Theologian Karl Barth echoed his sentiment when he said, "To me, the fact of forgiveness is even more astonishing than the raising of Lazarus."

The first great need of every human being is the forgiveness of his sins. When I forgive someone who has sinned against me, I say among other things, "From this time forward, I refuse to let this deed be a factor between us." Forgiveness means that the offended person lets the offender off the hook and relinquishes all rights to compensation for the physical, emotional, material or financial wrong he suffered at his hands.

Sometimes the message of forgiveness is seen in strange surroundings. For example, in Kurt Vonnegut's novel, *Slaughterhouse Five*, the hero is an ex-prisoner of war who had witnessed one of history's most devastating fire bombings. He cannot endure the memory of the suffering caused by the massive air raid. So he fantasizes. He pictures the event as though seeing a movie running backward. Bombers full of holes and corpses and wounded men take off backward from their home base and fly, tail first, to the target area. As the planes hover over the rubble that was a city, bomb-bay doors open, and through a miraculous magnetism, raging fires shrink and bomb fragments lift out of the debris to ascend into fuselage bellies where they reassemble. Then they are flown, backward still, to their place of origin and dismantled. Finally, the people who had first made them bury the deadly components in the ground—in the author's words, "to hide them very cleverly so they would never hurt anybody again." Friends, this is the picture Martin Luther created of Divine forgiveness when he said that "God un-creates our sins." It is as if He puts the story of our sinful lives in reverse, and blots out the sin and His memory of it. God doesn't just wipe the slate clean—He throws it away!

The prodigal boy found that he would never lack for forgiveness from his father if he would honestly come to him and confess his sins, truly repenting of them.

Then he discovered that he would not want for *fellowship with his father*. Forgiveness is worthless if it only makes the forgiven person neutral, if it only creates a blank. Forgiveness "clears the decks" for fellowship between the offended and the offender. To seek only forgiveness is a very selfish lifestyle. In fact, it is doubtful that a person who remains so selfish as to only want his tracks covered will truly be forgiven. This boy said, "I will arise and go to my father." His first thought was not for the comforts of home or the benefits of the estate, but rather to return to his father. And when the restoration began, it was not conducted through intermediaries. The father himself "ran, and fell on his neck, and kissed him."

When a sinner comes home to God, God is thereafter on call to him. There will never be a "busy signal" on the prayer line between him and God. God is never "out of the office." The Father seeks fellowship with His children more than they seek fellowship with Him. They may "come boldly before the throne of grace, to obtain mercy (the necessity for imperfect saints) and find grace (the necessity for full supply) to help in time of need" (Hebrews 4:16). One word in that statement will reveal its greatness. The word translated "help" ("grace to *help* in time of need") is the word used for a rope or a chain employed to gird a vessel that is under pressure. It is the very word that is used in Acts 27:17 (in the chapter of the dramatic shipwreck of the boat that was transporting Paul to Rome), to describe the undergirding of Paul's ship.

The ship on which Paul was a prisoner was caught in a fierce storm and was about to be broken up by the winds and waves. As a last resort the sailors wrapped huge chains around the hull of the ship to help hold it together. In the same way that those sailors strengthened their ship to keep it from cracking up, so Christ strengthens us to withstand the storms of temptation, trial, and daily demand. Without His help, His support, we too would crack up. And it is our fellowship with Him and His fellowship with us at "the throne of grace" that makes these supporting chains of Divine grace available to us.

Then, the returning son realized, "I shall not want for *food.*" He had left his father's table for the "fast foods" of the far country, but then had been reduced to husks in the pigsty. However, he had not even reached his father's house when the father ordered the household servants to "bring hither the fatted ('grain-fattened') calf" in order that the entire household might "eat and be merry."

Let the refugee from the far country hear this carefully. When you realize that the foods of the far country are no better for you than "husks that swine eat," when you decide to go back home where you are truly wanted by your Heavenly Father, you will discover that He has "bread enough and to spare" to feed your starving soul. You will never want for the rich foods of Heavens' Pantry when you come back to the Father's House.

The prodigal also made this discovery: "I will never want for *fullness of life* as long as I remain in my Father's house." His plea, "I have sinned," was met by the Father's command, "Bring

The Outrageous Love of God

forth the best robe and put it on him." He said, "I am not worthy to be called your son," but the father said, "Put a ring on his hand." He requested, "Make me as one of your hired servants," and the father answered, "Put shoes on his feet." Each of these endowments shows a restored franchise to this wayward son.

Good news! Each of these endowments also stands for some gift the Father in Heaven gives to His homecoming children. The robe represents the white robe of Christ's righteousness woven on the looms of Heaven to cover the sin and wretchedness of a sinner when he trusts Christ. The ring represents the covenant establishment of an eternal relationship between the Father, the "party of the first part," and the trusting sinner, the "party of the second part." The endless circle of the ring reveals that the relationship is unending, that it will never be broken. The shoes represent the placement of the returning son into the full position and privileges of a son in the household. Slaves went barefoot, but sons in the family wore shoes provided by the father. In short, the boy knew that every need was covered and that every necessity would be met in the future. He would never want fullness of life.

He discovered, finally, that he would never want *a happy future*. The father said, "Let us be merry." And the story closes with the words, "And they *began* to be merry," as if to suggest that the joy and gratification would linger as long as the boy was in the household. They may even have had anniversary celebrations to remember his past restoration and to restate the pledge of a happy future.

Every sinner who truly trusts Christ and comes home to God is guaranteed a happy future. The story will end, "And they lived happily ever after." Oh, family conflicts may arise along the way, misbehavior may momentarily darken the bright interior of the household, but the Father and his son are of such a disposition that they long to please each other. When the Father has his child on His heart, and the child has the Father in his, the future is certain.

We will leave the story where Jesus left it. They have only *begun* their adjustments in the Forever Family. "The best is yet to be." Now, go back to the first movement, the first point I have mentioned, in the story: "I want my share." *I* certainly do, don't *you*?

Focusing on the Father

Luke 15:20-24

I. His Love is a Parental, or Paternal, Love

    A. This accounts for the tenderness of His daily sympathy and supply

    B. This accounts for the terribleness of our sins

II. His Love is a Patient, or Persistent, Love

    A. The father was patiently waiting for his son's return

    B. The father was passionately wanting his son home

III. His Love is a Pardoning Love

    A. The father's posture

    B. The father's procedure

    C. The father's provision

Focusing on the Father

Luke 15:20-24

And he arose, and came to his father. But when he was yet a great way off, his father saw him, and had compassion, and ran, and fell on his neck, and kissed him. And the son said unto him, Father, I have sinned against heaven, and in thy sight, and am no more worthy to be called thy son. But the father said to his servants, Bring forth the best robe, and put it on him; and put a ring on his hand, and shoes on his feet: And bring hither the fatted calf, and kill it; and let us eat, and be merry: For this my son was dead, and is alive again; he was lost, and is found. And they began to be merry.

There are three main figures in the parable—the prodigal son, the elder brother, and the father. The one who receives the most of our attention is the prodigal son; the one who receives the second largest amount of our attention is the elder brother, and strangely, the forgotten figure in the parable is the father. However, when this parable is read as Jesus intended it, the dominant figure is the father. The prodigal son represents the person whose life is stained by the obvious sins; the elder brother represents the person who is shut out of the father's house because of pride and self-righteousness; the father represents God. Seldom does the Bible present such a clear picture of God's great love for sinners as when it paints the action of the father in welcoming the sinful

The Outrageous Love of God

son home from the far country. From this parable, we receive a clear impression of God's love for us. Look at the picture.

I. A Parental, or Paternal, Love

First, Jesus taught us to think of God's love as a *paternal* kind of love. It is like the love of a tender and compassionate father for his children. It was left for Jesus to make this revelation of God's love to us. In the Old Testament, the Bible suggests that God is like a father only about six times. For example, in Psalm 103:13, the Bible says, "Like as a *father* pities ... so the *Lord* pities." But references like this are few and far between in the Old Testament. These references are coupled with some excellent pictures of fatherhood in the Old Testament to give us a dim early image of what God is really like.

For example, when you hear the cry of Jacob from the book of Genesis, "Ye have bereft me of my children: Joseph is not, Simeon is not, and now you will take Benjamin from me," you have an excellent illustration of God the Father crying out in His great tenderness over the lost. Or when you hear David exclaiming, "Oh, Absalom, Absalom, my son, my son! Would God I had died for thee," you have just a hint of the feeling of God's heart about the lost ones for whom His Son *has* died. These early pictures and references to fatherhood give us a vision of the real nature of God.

But when you come to the New Testament, Jesus takes this great word, "Father," and makes it the concept in which we frame our thoughts about God. Jesus never lets us forget the word, "Father." He never preached a sermon without using that word. He never uttered a prayer without the word "father" being at the head of it. The first sentence recorded in the Bible from the lips of Jesus is this: "Know ye not that I must be about my Father's business?" His last words on the Cross were these: "Father, into thy hands I commend my spirit." Thus, throughout His ministry, Jesus attempted to impress upon men the fact that Almighty God is like a father in His dealings with us, and that His love is the love of the Divine Father for His children.

It is this fact—the fact that God loves us like a father—that accounts for the *tenderness* of His daily *sympathy* and supply for our lives. God has watched over every one of us *with* a Father's love and care all of our lives. He has arranged this world to accommodate us and our needs. He has supplied our wants, and surrounded us with pleasures and gratifications. He has hand-led us and spoon-fed us. He has protected us from dangers, and endured all of our waywardness and sins. And above all, He has given His Son to bring eternal life within our reach, and to raise us to the full position of Divine sonship. His care for you has been like the daily care of a father for His children. James 1:17 says that "every good and perfect gift is from above, and has come down from the Father of lights, in whom there is no vari-ableness, neither shadow of turning."

However, it is this fact, also, that reveals the *terribleness* of our *sins*. The fact that our sins are committed against a Divine *Father* is what makes our sins so terrible. When the prodigal son returned home, he made his confession in these words: "Father,

I have sinned against heaven, and in thy sight." It is the word, "father," in that confession that makes his sin such a criminal thing. Remove the word "father" from this sentence, and his sin is immediately much less serious than it was before. Let him pray, "Oh, Sovereign King, I have sinned against thee," and somehow the seriousness of the sin seems lessened. Or let him pray, "Oh, Judge of all, I have sinned against thee," and though that confession is serious, it is not as terrible as the other. But let him say and feel, "Father, I have sinned against thee and thy fatherly love," and we begin to see how grievous sin really is. And friend, your sins and mine are not just acts of wrong which we commit in isolation. Every sin we commit is a direct attack upon the fatherly heart of God. Every sin—whether indifference, pride, lack of loyalty to Christ, or whatever—is committed in direct violation of God's Divine Love. Every sin is a slap of God's face, *a stab into God's heart.*

Dr. W. H. Aitken, preacher of the past, was preaching in special evangelistic services in a large town. A young man came before the service one evening and said to Dr. Aitken, "When I went home last night after the service, I took my Bible and began to read the story you preached about last night. I hadn't read very far when I came to the words, 'Father, I have sinned against heaven and in thy sight, and am no more worthy to be called thy son;' and I can tell you, those words fairly broke my heart in two. I lay awake on my bed just sobbing, for I don't know how long, repeating those words over and over again: 'Father, I have sinned.'" What heart-breaking pathos and emotion there is in that confession! "Father, I have sinned—I have sinned against your heart and against your love!" *What a doubly damnable thing sin must be—to be committed against a father, and such a Father as this! To be committed against God, and such a God as this! To be committed against love, and such a Love as this!* God's love for you is a paternal kind of love—the love of a father for his children.

II. A Patient, or Persistent, Love

Second, Jesus taught us to think of God's love as a *patient* kind of love. Sometimes we over-dramatize the story of the prodigal son in the far country. We turn our imaginations loose in picturing the bright lights, the dance halls and theaters, the gambling houses and dens of shame. In lurid detail, we follow the prodigal in his downward plunge into the hog pen. So vivid is our imagination that we can almost feel the mud sucking at his feet in the pig sty, or hear the rustling of the dried husks as he gathers them to cast a meal to the hogs. And our attention is so taken up with the wretched misery of the poor prodigal that we forget everything else in the story.

But what about his father? What was *he* doing as the days gave way to months, and the slow years followed in their train? We are not specifically told in so many words what the father was doing, but there is no question in the minds of those who have carefully read the story. The fact that he saw the son from "a great way off" when he came back home indicates what he had been doing during the interval between the going away and the return. The years roll away, but the father doesn't, and can't, forget the wandering son. His love is slow to die. It does not matter how far away that boy has gone, the parent can never, never bury his love. Think what the young prodigal lost in all those years. He lost his home, his friends, his money, his position, his human dignity, and everything else he had—even his sanity. But there is one thing he did not lose for one minute in all those years—he never lost his father's love.

E. Stanley Jones tells the story of a young girl who left home, became lost in the life of a large city, and finally ended up in a house of shame. The news of her circumstances finally reached her mother back home. With a heavy heart, she set out to find her daughter. She took with her a number of her own photographs, and left one in each of the houses she visited. The girl came in one evening, glanced carelessly at the front table, and saw her mother's picture. On the front of the picture were written three words, "Come home," and it was signed, "Mother." Under the emotional impact of this loving appeal, the young woman fled the place, and there was a happy homecoming in her parent's home that same week. It was the same way in the story of the prodigal son. The image of his father was always with the son, pleading for him to come home.

Now, will you remind yourself that this father in this parable represents *God*? He loves you with a patient and persistent love. He has stood in the doorway of His own home patiently agonizing over you as you proudly and indifferently wander farther from Him in the far country. And He loves you through all your wanderings. He said, in Jeremiah 31:3, "I have loved you with an everlasting love, and with loving kindness have I drawn you unto myself."

In Old Testament days, the Israelite people had before them a constant and unending reminder of God's eternal love for man. In the center of their worship was an altar, and their law said, "The fire shall always be burning upon the altar; it shall never go out." That eternal flame was to the understanding worshiper a symbol of the patient and undying love of God for man. You see, dear friend, the light is always on in the window of the Father's House. You may have been gone a long time; you may have strayed far away from the Father's Hand, the Father's Heart, and the Father's Home, but *the Father wants you home*. Has it ever dawned on you what you've been doing to God all these years that you have refused Him? His heart bleeds love for your soul, but you shun Him and trample that love. And yet He patiently and persistently loves you still.

What pain and loneliness there is in this picture of God's love. What limitations God has imposed upon Himself in loving you. By the very nature of His love, He cannot rush off into the far country and drag you home. Because He has chosen it this way, He is forced to stand at the gate and patiently long for you to come home.

Dr. Henry Alford Porter tells a striking illustration of this truth. He says that he knew a businessman in St. Louis whose wife suddenly and unaccountably went insane. He was so devoted to her that he gave up his business and bestowed all of his time upon her. After months of his personal care, she still showed no signs of improvement. The family doctor suggested that he take his wife back to the mountains of east Tennessee, where she had been raised, and possibly the familiar surroundings would restore her sanity and bring back her reason. But, after months of waiting in the surroundings of her early home, she still remained mentally unbalanced. The husband, completely discouraged, finally brought her back to their home in St. Louis. He put her to bed the first night at home, and she immediately fell into a sound sleep. When she opened her eyes the next morning, her husband knew instantly that she was herself again. She exclaimed, "Where have I been, darling?" He quietly replied, "Honey, you've been on a long journey and now you're home again." She tried to remember, but didn't succeed, and finally asked, "And where have you been all the time I was gone?" With voice cracking with emotion, the husband replied, "I've been right here, waiting for you to come back." We, too, have gone on an insane journey into the far country, but God has patiently waited through the years—and is waiting for some of us still, to come back home to Him. His love is a patient love.

III. A Pardoning Love

Finally, Jesus taught us in this parable to think of God's love as a *pardoning* and forgiving love. After the prodigal had come to himself in the far country and had arisen to return to his father, as he approaches the old homestead, every word of the story from that point on breathes out God's pardoning love. The story says that the "father saw" the son "when he was yet a great way off." And you may rest assured, modern prodigal, that an eye no less keen and a look no less compassionate is fixed on you at this moment. If you are without Christ, you are indeed "a great way off" from God, and these words are the more terrible when you realize that the measurement of the distance is taken from *God's* standpoint, and He says you are "a great way off." But He sees you in spite of the distance. Looking through the telescope of His love, God sees you at this moment. And then the story says, "He had compassion, and ran, and fell on his neck, and kissed him." Remember that this is a picture of God drawn by Him who knows God best. Jesus pictures God *running*—God in a *hurry*—to welcome a sin-stained prodigal returning from the far country. This is the only time in the Bible God is ever pictured as being in a hurry. This dramatically illustrates His *willingness*—yes, His *eagerness*—to receive repenting sinners who come to Him. In Isaiah 55:6, the Bible says, "Seek ye the Lord while He may be found, call upon Him while He is near. Let the wicked forsake his way, and the unrighteous man his thoughts, and let him return unto the Lord, and He will have mercy upon him, and to our God, for He will abundantly pardon." *All* sinners need an *abundant* pardon, and such a pardon is clearly available.

"He ran, and fell on his neck, and kissed him." That one kiss of fatherly love obliterated and erased all the sins of the past and the memory of those sins. And then began the great process of restoration. As the father and the son are locked in each other's arms, from the middle of the roadway, the father gives the orders that will restore this prodigal boy to the full position of complete sonship in his home.

"Bring forth the best robe," he says, for it is unthinkable that a son should wear rags. And even so, when a repenting sinner comes to God the Father through Christ the Son, God clothes him in "the best robe," the garment of His righteousness, woven on the looms of Heaven, and thus makes him worthy to live in God's Presence forever.

"Put a ring on his hand." The ring is the symbol of an unbroken union between two parties in which those two parties become as one. When a sinner comes to Christ, he is united to God in an unbreakable union.

"And shoes on his feet." Only the slaves went barefoot. The shoes were a sign of sonship.

"And bring hither the fatted calf, and kill it; and let us eat, and be merry." Just a few days before, he was gnawing at the husks the swine did eat, but now the banquet table is loaded with delicacies for him. And the sinner who is starving his soul in sin little knows what a feast awaits him when he comes home to God.

Incidentally, have you noticed that after the father gives the orders for the reception of the son, that the son doesn't speak another word in this story? This suggests that his heart was so full of gratitude and his voice so choked with emotion that his lips were struck dumb and he could not speak.

And the story closes with the words, "And they began to be merry." Don't miss that word "merry." The boy thought he was having a good time when he was in the far country—laughing and playing frivolously, "having a ball." But now he sees that his laughter there was only a hollow hint of real laughter and real joy. And don't forget that word, "began." "They *began* to be merry. This means that the joy I have in Christ now—the joy of forgiveness and pardon, the joy of salvation, the joy of fellowship with Him—is only a beginning. The joy will deepen, the rapture will increase, the music will become sweeter, until the heavenly feast lies spread before us. Oh, the pardoning love of God! That love is reaching forth to you at this hour. It is a *prodigal* (extravagant) love. Can you continue to stay away from a Father who loves you like that?

The Elder Brother

Luke 15:25-32

I. Ungrateful to His Father
    A. The father's provision

    B. The son's perversion

II. Unappreciative of His Fortune
    A. His inheritance

    B. His indifference

III. Unhappy with His Fate
    A. He did the father's work with his hands

    B. He did not do the father's will from his heart

IV. Unforgiving Toward His Fallen Fellow
    A. He didn't consider his brother

    B. He didn't claim his brother

    C. He didn't communicate with his brother

The Elder Brother

Luke 15:25-32

Now his elder son was in the field: and as he came
and drew nigh to the house, he heard music and danc-
ing. And he called one of the servants, and asked
what these things meant. And he said unto him, Thy
brother is come; and thy father hath killed the fatted
calf, because he hath received him safe and sound. And
he was angry, and would not go in: therefore came
his father out, and entreated him. And he answering
said to his father, Lo, these many years do I serve thee,
neither transgressed I at any time thy commandment;
and yet thou never gavest me a kid, that I might make
merry with my friends: But as soon as this thy son was
come, which hath devoured thy living with harlots, thou
hast killed for him the fatted calf. And he said unto him,
Son, thou art ever with me, and all that I have is thine.
It was meet that we should make merry, and be glad:
for this thy brother was dead, and is alive again; and
was lost, and is found.

Luke fifteen could be called "the chapter of lost things." There
are four lost things in the chapter (not merely three, as most
readers think). There are a lost sheep, a lost coin, and two lost
sons in the chapter. We don't normally think of the elder brother
as lost because he stayed home (however, we must remember

that the lost coin in verses 8-10 was lost *in the house*). But the one thing that we don't normally *consider* to be lost was, in fact, *so* lost that when the story is concluded, *he is the only one who remains lost*.

A reader of the great four-part parable (verse 3) in Luke fifteen might well wish that the long parable had ended with the prodigal boy's return and the banquet that celebrated that return. The words, "And they began to be merry," would have provided a quite pleasing conclusion. The additional story of the elder brother bathes the entire parable in an atmosphere of gloom and leaves that atmosphere hanging around the heart of the reader. However, the elder brother is the actual reason for telling the parable to begin with. The key to the interpretation of the entire chapter is found in the first two verses, "Then drew near unto him all the publicans and sinners for to hear him. And the Pharisees and scribes murmured, saying, This man receiveth sinners, and eateth with them." The long parable begins at verse three, and verse three opens with the word "and," which connects the parable closely with those first two verses. The "publicans and sinners" of verse one could well be represented by the first three lost things, but the "Pharisees and scribes of verse two are unquestionably represented by the fourth "lost thing" in the story, the elder brother. So the story was provoked by the murmuring of the Pharisees and scribes against Jesus because of the gracious reception He gave the publicans and sinners. If the account of the elder brother had been omitted, the story would have failed to fulfill its purpose.

When you look at the profile of the elder brother presented in the story, you can understand and appreciate the petition of the little boy who prayed, "Lord, make all the bad people good, *and make all the good people nice*." It really was fortunate that the elder brother was in the field when the prodigal returned, so that he encountered his father first. If he had met his brother first, he might have been tempted to return to the far country and his riotous living!

You see, the elder brother was also a lost son. He was living in the *spirit* of the far country, even if he had not made the long trip! He was as far from his father's *heart* as the younger son was from his father's *house*. Distance is the least among the things that separate us from God and from one another. We can eat at the same table with our brothers, and sit in the same pew, and still be continents apart in attitude and spirit.

Years ago, I read a book that had in it chapters entitled, "The Publican In Us," "The Prostitute In Us," "The Prodigal In Us," and "The Pharisee (Elder Brother) In Us." In the fullest and most terrible sense, every human being has all four of these people in him. When I look inside of myself in an honest moment, I can detect all four of these sinners. And the ugliest one of the bunch is the elder brother! My intolerance of others is intolerable! My judgmental spirit needs to be judged and cast out!

It is interesting that while the prodigals sometimes have a difficult time getting into our churches, the elder brothers are frequently elected to our official boards and committees, and (I speak from experience) often occupy the pulpits of our churches!

The tragedy of the elder brother was that he had *no adequate and honest sense of personal sin, no uneasy stirring of conscience, and no desperation of soul.* He assumed the inferiority of his brother, and thus, he necessarily assumed his own superiority. But here are some basic questions: What produces elder brothers? What makes highly privileged saints turn into elder brothers? Why does the elder brother lurk so near to the surface all the time in each of us? What traits, if unchecked, will always turn the saints of God into elder brothers?

I. Ungrateful to His Father

First, it must be noted that, though he stayed at home and resided in his father's house, he had hidden within him a heart that was *ungrateful to his father*. In stead of being *grateful* for what he *had*, he was *ungrateful* for what he *didn't have*. So ingratitude is the first producer of the kind of people who have the attitude of the elder brother.

Note how this man treated his father. In verse 29, he spoke to his father without the courtesy of even addressing him. This affront was unheard of in the Middle East, and is surely intentional in the story as a symptom of the boy's heart. Also, the boy forced the father to come outside the house if they were to talk. This is a sulking way to control his father and register his protest against his younger brother. When the father and the elder brother did talk, the elder brother expressed a doubt of his father's generosity: "Lo, these many years ." He treated his *father* like a mere *employer*—and he was very proud of the service he had rendered to his father.

In contrast, note how the *father* treated *him*. Verse 28 says, "His father came out and entreated him." Remember, this is a *patriarchal* society! The father's prerogative was to *command*, *not* to *reason* with a protesting son.

It is evident that this son was not thankful to his father for any of the things the father had provided for him. Thankfulness is an antidote for any dispositional, negative sin. But this boy was not thankful. Sooner or later, the attitude of ingratitude to the Father will make any Christian insensitive to his brothers or sisters—and he will become an elder brother.

Years ago, a fine pastor who is a friend of mine said to me, "Herb, I fear that Southern Baptists have *become* the elder brother!" May God have mercy upon me—and upon us! While daily loaded with God's benefits (Psalm 68:19), while buried under an avalanche of His blessings, we can be so ungrateful that we reveal all the symptoms of the elder brother!

II. Unappreciative of His Fortune

Second, this man built an "elder brother disposition" by being *unappreciative of his fortune.*

In verse 29, he said to his father, "Lo, these many years do I serve thee, neither transgressed I at any time thy commandment; and yet thou never gavest me a kid, that I might make

The Outrageous Love of God

merry with my friends." The father answered (verse 31), "Son, thou art ever with me, and all that I have is thine."

Since this boy was the elder of two sons, he would inherit two-thirds of his father's estate when the father died. And he had access to all of the estate while the father lived. So he could negotiate a large fortune.

The same is true of every Christian. Whether the saints "cash in" on their treasure or not, each saint is fabulously rich. Romans 8:17 says that the Christian is "an heir of God, and a joint-heir with Christ." Ephesians 1:3 says that "God has already blessed us with all spiritual blessings in heavenly places in Christ." Romans 8:32 says, "If God spared not His own Son, but delivered Him up for us all, how shall He not with Him freely give us *all things*?" In other words, if God gave us the Big Blessing when He gave us Jesus, can He not be counted on to give us all lesser blessings as well? If He gave us the Great Gift, surely He will give us the wrapping paper and ribbon as well. I Timothy 7:17 says, "God has given us richly all things to enjoy." And I Corinthians 3:21-23 says, "All things are yours . . . all are yours, and you are Christ's, and Christ is God's." That is, if *you* truly belong to *Christ, all things truly* belong to *you*.

Years ago, I happened upon a copy of one volume of *Macauley's Essays on British History* in a used book store. One illustration made the difficult reading worthwhile. In the essay entitled "Lord Clive" (the British-appointed prime minister of India when India was a British colony), the account is given of the accusation against Clive of embezzling a fabulous fortune from the princes of India. The account tells of his indictment and his return to India and the trial he faced there. During the trial, Clive both testified and defended himself. Macauley wrote, "Clive was subjected to the most unsparing examination and cross-examination." Macaulay also expressed this opinion about Clive, "The boldness and ingeniousness of his replies would alone suffice to show how alien from his nature were the frauds to which, in the course of his eastern negotiations, he had sometimes descended." Then the book brilliantly records Clive's defense. "He admitted that he had received immense sums from the princes, but he denied that, in doing so, he had violated any obligation of morality or honor. He described in vivid language the situation in which his victory had placed him; great princes were dependent on his pleasure; wealthy bankers were bidding against each other for his smiles. The treasure coffers of India were thrown wide open, and 'I was invited to help myself, to take as much as I wanted. Vaults piled with gold and jewels were thrown open to me alone. Is it possible that I only took 200,000 pounds? Great God, Mr. Chairman, at this moment I stand before you astonished at my own moderation! I am amazed that I took so little!'"

The elder brother belittled his fortune by being unappreciative of it, and so do we. The Bible gives a classic illustration of this sin in the story of King Ahab and Naboth's vineyard. You will recall that the small landholder Naboth stood firm in the face of the King's demand that he sell the property to the King. "I will not give thee my vineyard," he said, and this refusal provoked both depression and anger in the King's heart. When Jezebel, Ahab's queen, found him sulking like a child and learned the reason for his behavior, she chided him with the words, "Dost thou now govern the Kingdom of Israel?" (I Kings 21:6, 7). She meant that Ahab had the right as king to commandeer Naboth's vineyard as he wished, but here words contain an unconscious irony: *Why all this fuss over a mere vineyard when you have a whole kingdom that is yours?* That story and the similar story of the elder brother reveal how desperately easy it is for the soul with a grievance to lose all sense of proportion. Instead of appreciation, we are easily filled with apprehension because of the wrong treatment we think we have received. The elder brother was hacked off about a baby goat (or at lease so he said); what would you or I need before we would behave ourselves like grown-up, mature Christians, instead of spiritual babies? As we so often are, this boy was unappreciative of his large fortune, and so he declined into protest and provides for us today the classic profile of "an elder brother" believer.

III. Unhappy with His Fate

Third, this boy became a dispirited, aggravated, negative elder brother because he was *unhappy with his fate*. Though he had every advantage and should have been a joyful participant both in the work of the estate and in the welcome-home party for his younger brother, instead he was a *sour* son because he was discontented over the treatment he was receiving in his father's house. In short, though he was *diligent* and *obedient*, he was not *radiant*. He had no joy, no contentment, no buoyancy, no enthusiasm. As Mark Twain said about such a person, "He was a good man in the worst sense of the word."

This elder brother proves that it is possible to do the Father's *work* without doing the Father's *will*. He was doing the job because he *had* to, not because he *got* to. His motto was not, "I *get* to do it," but rather, "I've *got* to do it." He had a "hidden agenda" beneath the surface of his life. He is typical of multitudes of workers in all fields who go through the motions, do their work, pay their bills, raise their families—but always with a "hidden agenda." The Biblical goal for Christian service is stated in Ephesians 6:;6, "Doing the will of God *from the heart;* with *good will* doing service, as to the Lord, and not to man." I was driving home from a series of meetings in the Carolinas and heard a song on a Christian country music station which had this key line, "Lord, please let me *do your will* so I won't *get in your way*." The elder brother looked like he was doing his father's will, but his attitude finally proved that he was actually getting in his father's way. And one of the reasons was that he was unhappy with his fate.

IV. Unforgiving Toward His Fallen Fellow

Finally, this man created the Biblical profile of an "elder brother" by being *unforgiving toward his fallen fellow*. Verses 27-30 record this exchange: "And he (one of the household servants) said unto him (the elder brother), Thy brother is come; and thy father hath killed the fatted calf, because he hath received him safe and sound. And he was angry, and would not go in: therefore came his father out, and entreated him. And he answering said to his father, Lo, these many years do I serve thee, neither transgressed I at any time thy commandment; and yet thou never gavest me a kid, that I might make merry with my friends: But as soon as this thy son was come, which hath devoured thy living with harlots, thou hast killed for him the fatted calf."

What was it that convinced the younger son to go home? It was *the generosity of the father!* In verses 17 and 18, we read his sensible soliloquy: "And when he came to himself, he said, How many hired servants of my father's have bread enough and to spare, and I perish with hunger! I will arise and go to my father." Romans 2:4 asks, "Do you despise the riches of God's goodness and forebearance and longsuffering; not knowing that the goodness of God leaders you to repentance?" The elder brother had been the constant recipient of his father's goodness, but he had only been further hardened by it. The younger son, on the other hand, was reminded of his father's goodness and forebearance and longsuffering while in the degradation of the far country, and he was attracted by it. The love that melted the heart of the younger brother hardened the heart of the elder brother.

It is tragic that the welcome-home party for the younger son was already in progress when the elder brother found out about it. This suggests how far removed he really was from the sentiment and sensitivity of the father's heart.

Note the sad progression. First, the elder brother didn't *consider* his brother. He had never interceded for him while he was in the far country, nor had he made any move whatever to get him back home again.

My wife and I have just finished reading the child's classic boy-and-dog story entitle *Shiloh*. It is another of those child's classics that should be read and discussed in an adult group because of its ethical issues. The book contains these two revealing paragraphs:

"You know, Marty," Ma said, "Dara Lynn don't know who ate the ear off her candy rabbit and I don't know who did it, but Jesus knows. And right this very minute Jesus is looking down with the saddest eyes on the person who ate that chocolate. The Bible says that the worst thing that can ever possibly happen to us is to be separated forever from God's love. I hope you'll keep that in mind."

I just swallowed and didn't say anything. But before I went to bed, when Ma asked me again about that rabbit, I gulped and said yes, and she made me get down on my knees and ask God's forgiveness, which wasn't so bad. I honestly felt better afterward. But then she said that Jesus wanted me to go in the next room and tell Dara Lynn what I'd done, and Dara Lynn had a fit all over again. Threw a box of Crayolas at me and could have broke my nose. Called me a rotten, greedy pig. If *that* made Jesus sad, Ma never said.

The Outrageous Love of God

In this case, it is the "elder sister" spirit that is expressed. And though the obvious wrong (like that of the prodigal son) is recognized and condemned, the sin of the "elder sister" (as is often sadly true) is ignored. Like the elder brother of Luke 15, Dara Lynn did not give proper consideration to her brother in the time of his moral "homecoming."

Second, he didn't *claim* his brother. In verse 30, he sarcastically called him "this thy son" when addressing his father, instead of calling him "my brother." How tragic it is when one natural brother in a family cannot acknowledge another. And how tragic it is when a Christian brother cannot acknowledge another brother in the same spiritual family. There is great power in the loving acknowledgment of a brother.

But what an incredibly powerful force is released into human life when a holy and loving person calls a conspicuous sinner, "My Brother!" One of the great stories from the legendary life of Francis of Assissi concerned a moment on a country road when Francis was traveling by horseback. He came upon a leper beside the road. The leper called out, "Please, sir, could you give me a gift?" Francis reigned in his horse, turned back, dismounted beside the beggar, embraced and kissed him and said, "I'm sorry, brother, but I have nothing to give you." The beggar replied, "Oh, but sir, you have given me the greatest gift of all!" Francis replied, "The greatest gift of all? Why, man, I have given you nothing." "Oh, but you have, sir. You gave me the greatest gift of all—*you called me Brother*!"

But note that entrenched self-righteousness cannot give such a gift; settled self-righteousness cannot make such an admission. The elder brother did not claim his own brother. He cynically spoke of him to his father as "this thy son" instead of "this my brother."

Third, he didn't *communicate* with his brother. He didn't offer a word or a gesture of welcome, but only isolated himself in sulking protest. His sentiment was, *"He will have to apologize to me before I will acknowledge him."* What a strange twist! In the perverted heart of this self-righteous prig, his brother's sin, repentance and restoration were all just one big affront to him personally! Like Shylock in Shakespeare's *Merchant of Venice*, he was so offended that he demanded his "pound of flesh" before his grievance could be appeased.

How much time do Christians waste in building walls when they could be building bridges? And those walls are so quickly set in cement!

Turn to Galatians 5:22-23 and read the list of "the fruit of the Spirit." "Love, joy, peace, long-suffering, gentleness, goodness, faith, meekness, and temperance." Note that the elder brother lacked all nine characteristics. But what about me? What about you? How lacking am I, or how full am I, of the fruit of the Spirit? Someone wisely said, "You will never recommend the Bread of Life to anyone else if you look as if that food disagrees with you." The elder brother is the prototype of the "sour saint" who is so self-centered that he can only grieve over his supposed mistreatment. He can't even celebrate the providence that has drowned him with blessings, let alone the gracious restoration of a mis-spent brother.

My all-time favorite novel is *Les Miserables*, written by the great French writer, Victor Hugo. In substance, the novel is overtly Christian, though heavily colored by Roman Catholic theology. I have seen several movie versions of the great work, and each tells the story in a moving way. However, my favorite version is the video of the musical done in Royal Albert Hall in London. Though it omits some "lesser parts" of the story, it vividly por-trays the great struggle between law (represented by constable Javert) and grace (pictured in the Bishop and in the conversion and noble life of Jean Valjean, the transformed ex-convict). The musical vividly pictures (as does the movie) the conversion of Jean Valjean under the impact of the Bishop's mercy and grace. In Jean Valjean's soliloquy of self-examination and repentance, he sings,

"What have I done? Sweet Jesus, what have I done?
Become a thief in the night! Become a dog on the run.
And have I fallen so far, And is the hour so late?
My life was a war that could never be won.

They gave me a number and murdered Valjean
When they chained me and left me for dead
Just for stealing for a starving child a mouthful of bread.
Yet why did I allow this man To touch my soul and teach
me love?

He treated me like any other. He gave me his trust, he called
me Brother!

My life he claims for God above. Can these things be?"

The climax of his conversion is reached when he adds:

"I'll escape now from the world, From the world of Jean
Valjean.

Jean Valjean is nothing now, Another story must begin."

You can easily locate yourself in that story and in the story
told by Jesus in Luke 15. At this very moment, you may be
Jean Valjean, the sinner before conversion. Or you may be Jean
Valjean, the saint just after conversion (and still engulfed in the
battle between flesh and Spirit). Or you may be becoming Jean
Valjean, the saintly servant who is ever growing in grace and
kindly serving others. Or you may be more like Constable Javert,
the self-righteous man who can never adjust to the grace-life of
the new-born Christian, but always remembers only the sin-life
of the individual before he met Christ. But the entire secret of
life is in the realization that Jesus became the Brother of all men
through his incarnation, saves those who will repent and trust
Him and calls them "Brother" through their new birth, and even
offers the same possibilities to the Elder Brothers of life! Friend,
look at your Big Brother, Jesus, leave behind your "Elder Brother
self," and enter the most Blessed Brotherhood ever known to
man. *"He gave me His trust; He called me Brother."* Can I do less
for others than He has done for me?

If you are without Christ, hear again the words of Jean Valjean: "My old life is nothing now; *a new story must begin.*" You can have a brand new life, a brand new heart, a brand new beginning! How? Turn from your self-trust and your sins, receive Jesus Christ and trust Him to come into your life, forgive your sins, give you the gift of eternal life, and change you into the true brother you were meant to be.

Lost Things in Luke 15
A Summary Study

There are four lost things in Luke 15: a sheep, a silver coin, and two sons. This chart will suggest some of the developing ideas which may be detected in the four stories.

Sheep	Silver	Son #1	Son #2
Minimum of will	Minimum of will	Maximum of will	Maximum of will
Lost through weakness	Lost through carelessness	Lost through wickedness	Lost through willfulness
Exemplifies "iniquity"	Exemplifies "sin"	Exemplifies "transgression"	Exemplifies "trespass"
The *instinctive* sinner	The *insensible* sinner	The *insane* sinner	The *insensitive* sinner
Represents the sinner who lives *stupidly*	Represents the sinner who lives *sluggishly*	Represents the sinner who lives *sinfully*	Represents the sinner who lives *selfishly*
A warning against living an *animal* life	A warning against living a *mechanical* life	A warning against living a *volitional* life	A warning against living a *dispositional* life
The danger of careless *drifting*	The danger of careless *dislocation*	The danger of corrupt *disobedience*	The danger of cynical *disposition*

A few words of explanation about the above chart. In the first line of comparison, the first two objects, the sheep and the silver coin, have a minimum of will. The sheep has little strength of will, and the coin, being dead, has no will at all. However, in the stories of the two sons, each has a maximum of will. The prodigal son shows a stubborn and sinful will, while the elder brother shows a smug and self-righteous will.

In the second line of comparison, the sheep and the silver coin are typical of the sinner who is too weak to choose God, while the two sons are too wicked to live in relationship with Him.

In the third line, four of the distinctive Biblical words for moral evil are used and defined. The word "iniquity" defines the inward character twist, the moral distortion every man experiences within, the "bent" of human nature toward sin. This "twist" was locked into man through the Fall of Adam. This aspect of sin is seen in the sheep who has a "bent" toward straying. The word "sin" means "to miss the mark," and is pictured in the coin that is misplaced and out of circulation, and thus is failing to fulfill the purpose for which it was made. The word "transgression" means a deliberate crossing of boundaries—boundaries of law, of morality, of safety, of reason, etc. This is pictured in the rebellious and wretched younger brother, who deliberately wished evil upon his father (the inheritance was normally received by the heir upon the death of the father) in order to gain selfish benefit for himself. Further, the younger son then arrogantly crossed all bounds of right and reason to squander his resources in an unwise lifestyle. The fourth word for sin pictured in these stories is the word "trespass," the word for a "falling out of the way" which is not as noticeable as transgression, but has the same serious consequences in the end. This is seen in the account of the elder brother.

In the stories of the sheep and the silver, the emphasis is on the *sovereignty of God*. In the stories of the two sons, the emphasis is on the *responsibility of man*.

The stories of the two sons have different emphases: (1) Compassion for prodigals is presented in the story of the "prodigal" son; (2) Condemnation for Pharisees is presented in the story of the elder brother.

The fourth line of comparison examines the four "types" of sinners pictured in these four stories. The sheep represents the sinner who just "follows his drives," not knowing that these drives are pushing him step by step into deepening danger and finally to the brink of hell. The silver coin represents the insensible sinner. After all, a coin has no sense at all, no intelligence, being dead. The prodigal son represents the "insane" sinner. This may sound extravagant, but it is not. With everything considered—God, life, death, heaven, hell and eternity—a human being must be characterized by a measure of insanity if he omits God from his life. Indeed, the Bible says, "Madness is in man's heart while he lives." Then, the elder brother represents the insensitive sinner. He is numbed and deadened by his blatant self-righteousness, thus showing total insensitivity to his brother and to his father.

The fifth and sixth lines of comparison again suggest four kinds of sinners. The sheep represents the "dumb" sinner, the sinner who never stops to think about ultimate issues and drifts toward his doom. Here, Jesus warns us against an excessively animalistic lifestyle, one in which we just follow our animal drives. The silver coin represents the sinner who passively allows himself to fall into darkness and death. This is the sinner who lives mechanically, like a coin passively inserted into a slot by someone else's hand. The prodigal boy represents the sinner who is dominated by a rebellious will and must be broken by adversity and want. To most people, he is the one in the story who most looks like a "sinner." The elder brother represents the sinner who reveals his sin in the form of self-righteous superiority over others.

In the final line of comparison, Jesus warns us about four dangerous patterns that characterize all lost people and also may recur in the lives of truly saved people. These are the dangers of aimless drifting, purposeless dislocation from any true usefulness, passive or aggressive disobedience of the known will of God, and the cultivation of a cynical disposition toward other people.

Finally, the four stories may be divided into two categories. In the stories of the sheep and the silver coin, Jesus shows us how we are to *retrieve* lost people from their dangerous position and their deadly lifestyles. We are to aggressively go after them, snatching them as brands from the burning. Then, in the stories of the two brothers, Jesus reveals how lost people may

The Outrageous Love of God

be *received* by those who are "found" when they come home. One is the reception of the Father, the other the reception of the Pharisee. Is it possible that many more lost people don't come home to God because they have been led by experience to think that they would be given a Pharisee's cold reception instead of a loving Christian's open arms?

Above all, the four stories highlight the love of God. The *seeking and suffering* love of God is seen in the story of the shepherd seeking his one lost sheep. The *searching and scouring and singing* woman reveals the heart of God in His quest to find and rescue sinners. And the *summoning, suffering and singing* father represents God the Father who is always inviting sinners to fling themselves into His arms of love and find His great heart.

An old proverb says, "When the King stoops to pick up something, it must have value." Jesus the King of kings has stooped from Heaven's highest glory to earth's darkest gloom to pick you up and save you. You are worth a great deal to Him. Have you been saved? Have you surrendered your life to Him? Is He realizing an adequate return on the investment He has made in you?

Other titles by Herb Hodges

Tally Ho the Fox!

The Foundation for
Building World-Visionary,
World-Impacting,
Reproducing Disciples.

$7.95

Fox Fever

Exploring both the Will
and the Skill to obey Christ's
Great Commission to "turn
people into disciples."

$7.95